RISE OF
ISIS

A THREAT WE CAN'T IGNORE

JAY SEKULOW

WITH THE ACLJ LAW OF WAR TEAM
JORDAN SEKULOW, ROBERT W. ASH, AND DAVID FRENCH

HOWARD BOOKS

New York   Nashville   London   Toronto   Sydney   New Delhi

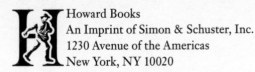

Howard Books
An Imprint of Simon & Schuster, Inc.
1230 Avenue of the Americas
New York, NY 10020

First Howard Books ebook edition September 2014
This Howard Books trade paperback edition June 2015
This Howard Books hardcover edition June 2015

HOWARD and colophon are trademarks of Simon & Schuster, Inc.

For information about special discounts for bulk purchases, please contact Simon & Schuster Special Sales at 1-866-506-1949 or business@simonandschuster.com.

The Simon & Schuster Speakers Bureau can bring authors to your live event. For more information or to book an event contact the Simon & Schuster Speakers Bureau at 1-866-248-3049 or visit our website at www.simonspeakers.com.

Interior design by Renato Stanisic
Cover design by Bruce Gore
Cover image by AFP PHOTO/HO/AL-FURQAN MEDIA

Manufactured in the United States of America

Library of Congress Cataloging-in-Publication Data

Sekulow, Jay.
    The rise of ISIS : the coming massacre / by Jay Sekulow ; with the ACLJ Law of War Team, Jordan Sekulow, Robert W. Ash, and David French.
        pages cm
    1. ISIS (Terrorist organization) 2. Terrorists--Irag. 3. Terrorists--Syria. 4. Terrorism--Religious aspects--Islam. 5. Terrorism--Middle East. I. Title.
    HV6433.172218574 2014
    956.05'4--dc23
                                        2014035291

10   9   8   7   6   5   4   3   2   1

ISBN 978-1-5011-2549-2 (hardcover)
ISBN 978-1-5011-2547-8 (pbk)
ISBN 978-1-5011-0515-9 (ebook)

The portions of this book describing the rise of ISIS and its military capabilities and describing Hamas, its history, and many of its tactics are adapted from a series of papers presented by Jay Sekulow in July 2014 at Oxford University's History, Politics, and Society program on Religion and Politics in the Middle East.

CONTENTS

FOREWORD

This past summer, I was privileged to participate in a number of informative discussions with members of the University of Oxford faculty regarding the current state of affairs in the Middle East. These conversations centered on the emerging threat to human values posed by ISIS and other groups. As a consequence my eyes have been opened wide to the bracing capacity of radical jihadists to engage in human savagery. Once exposed to evidence of brutality that includes the deliberate shooting of babies in the presence of their mothers, the rape of women who were then told that the only way to redeem their honor was to blow themselves up as suicide bombers, and the summary decapitation of men, women, and children when they failed to comply with conversion edicts issued by Caliph Ibrahim, the leader of the Islamic State, it becomes impossible to remain silent.

Given that ISIS poses an existential threat to a number of countries, including Israel, and represents a growing menace to lives of Yazidis, moderate Sunni Muslims, Shia Muslims, Kurds, Christians, and Jews, it is highly doubtful that anyone but the most naïve among us would believe that negotiations, led by the United Nations or anyone else, are the proper way forward. Instead, readers of this new book by Jay Sekulow and his team will discover that evil such as this must be met with force. Nothing else will do. Sekulow describes the origins of ISIS and its ideological links to other jihadists, and clarifies 1) the fractured relationship between ISIS, a radical jihadist group that was founded in Iraq and Syria and has directed its efforts toward the creation of an Islamic Caliphate, and al-Qaeda, which has oriented its terrorist attacks against Western and Arab governments, horrifically exemplified by the events of September 11, 2001; 2) the breathtakingly rapid advance of ISIS in Iraq, fueled by its striking commitment to terror, a development that has been fostered by the bewildering courage deficit of the Iraqi military forces; 3) the ideological and visionary links between ISIS and Hamas that combine to threaten Israel's existence; and 4) substantial evidence revealing how radical jihadist groups like ISIS pose a mounting threat to the American people. Adding urgency to Sekulow's analysis, a U.S. senator recently explained how radical jihadists have collected the components necessary to assemble a bomb to "blow up" a U.S. city.[1]

Given these developments, it bears noticing that the Enlightenment dream of inevitable human progress, grounded in the claim that we are all born free and equal in dignity and rights, and premised on hope that the arc of history bends toward justice, is now in tatters. This outcome fundamentally challenges Americans' endless pursuit of individualism and tolerance. Readers of this book will discover that in our postmodern era, certain things are indeed intolerable. The failure to face the facts richly addressed by the authors of *Rise of ISIS: A Threat We Can't Ignore* exposes democratic nations to the rising danger that they—perhaps misled by the persistent fecklessness of the United Nations and other institutions, which refuse to recognize the obvious threat to Western civilization posed by radical Islamist jihadists—will capitulate to the prospect of appeasement, disaster, and death. Capitulation will enable the murderous forces, which have already been unleashed in the Middle East, to expand their territory and reach by directly encroaching on the West. Hopefully readers of this vital book will be roused to prevent this from happening, in prelude to the pursuit of a durable peace in an epoch rife with persecution based on savage ethnic and religious intolerance, and short on reconciliation.

Harry G. Hutchison
Visiting Fellow, Harris Manchester College, University of Oxford
Professor, George Mason University School of Law

CHAPTER ONE

THE HORROR OF JIHAD

I t was the video no one wanted to see, that few people could bear to watch.

A young American, James Foley, was on his knees next to a masked, black-clad jihadist. The jihadist was holding a knife. Foley began reciting a prepared text—delivered under the ultimate duress—condemning America. When he finished, he visibly braced himself.

We all knew what was coming.

The Foley beheading video was too graphic for YouTube. Twitter banned users who tweeted its horrific images. And while few Americans actually watched the horrifying act, everyone knew what happened.

It was ISIS, a new and horrifying jihadist force that had been unleashed in the Middle East. And now they had slaughtered an American.

Except ISIS wasn't new. These horrible images weren't unusual. Some of us had seen them before.

. . . . .

The DVD was lying in the dust.

Still weary from a midnight air assault where they'd attacked enemy-held objectives for hours throughout the evening and early morning, the troopers of the Second ("Sabre") Squadron, Third Armored Cavalry Regiment almost missed the evidence as they searched an abandoned village south of Balad Ruz, Diyala Province, Iraq.

The village may have been abandoned, but people had recently been there. Clothes were scattered on floors, cars and trucks were still parked outside homes, and there was blood, lots of blood. And it seemed fresh.

It was a chilling sight. Soldiers stepped gingerly over children's sandals and little girls' dresses. They walked past bullet holes in walls, and they picked up cell phones left lying on tables in one- and two-room houses.

Our soldiers looked for anything that would provide a clue to the fate of the villagers, but the more experienced knew they were looking for one item in particular—a DVD.

In many ways, the DVD was a jihadist's calling card, his method of bragging about his deeds in the years before smartphones and instant YouTube uploads. Terrorists would compile "greatest hits" compilations, showing IED strikes on Americans, mass executions of Iraqis, and the detonation of suicide bombs. DVDs were so common that our soldiers were trained to expect an imminent attack if a civilian was spotted filming them with a video camera.

And there it was, in a courtyard, in plain view. The troopers picked it up and kept it safe until it could be airlifted out, along with fourteen terrorist detainees, to Forward Operating Base Caldwell, a small American base just miles from the Iranian border.

As soon as the DVD arrived, intelligence officers rushed it to their office, put it on computers set aside for reviewing terrorist material (which could always contain viruses or other malware), and started watching.

What they saw was nothing short of horrifying.

As with all jihadist videos, the camera work was shaky, and the sounds were chaotic and loud. While the cameraman yelled "Allahu Akhbar!" (God is great) into the microphone, a group of about thirty Iraqi men, women, and children were led at gunpoint into a field, a field our soldiers recognized as being near the abandoned village.

One by one, the Iraqis were separated from the group and placed in the middle of a small group of jihadists. The first one was a woman, not more than forty years old. As the camera zoomed in, she had a vacant, hopeless look in her eyes—a look of utter despair.

The shouts of "Allahu Akhbar!" intensified until they all blended into one long, loud cheer, like the frenzy after a goal is scored at a soccer match. Then—as the shouting reached its peak and the camera zoomed close—the terrorists beheaded the woman.

They didn't do it with a clean chop of a sword like one sees on television or in movies, but instead by sawing furiously through her neck with knives. It wasn't over immediately. As she choked on her own blood, the jihadists kept sawing, and sawing, and sawing.

Finally, they pulled her head off, waved it to the camera, shouted in victory, and motioned for the next terrified victim to come forward.

How do we know this event occurred—one the mainstream media never knew about or reported? Because one of the authors of this book, a member of the American Center for Law and Justice (ACLJ) Law of War team who was deployed to Iraq at the time, saw the video with his own eyes. He walked through the streets of that village himself, stepping over bloody clothes. And he remembers. In fact, he can never forget.

What was the name of that terrorist organization?

Al-Qaeda in Iraq, or AQI.

And after al-Qaeda rejected AQI because of tactics such as this, tactics so depraved and brutal that they even repulsed al-Qaeda leader Osama bin Laden, what did AQI become?

The Islamic State of Iraq and Syria.

It became ISIS.

The sirens were some of the loudest noises I'd ever heard. They blasted apart the stillness of the day, assaulted my eardrums, and made me involuntarily duck.

I was in Israel in 2008, just outside of the Hamas-held Gaza Strip. As chief counsel of the American Center for Law and Justice, I was there (along with my son and coauthor of this book, Jordan) to meet with Israeli officials to discuss a response to utterly frivolous claims that Israel's acts of self-defense against Hamas constituted "war crimes."

To help us make our case, I wanted to see Gaza with my own eyes, to see what life was like in southern Israel under rocket fire.

I got more than I bargained for.

When the warning siren went off, I knew I was safe. I was in a command bunker, meeting with key Israeli leaders. But my immediate thought wasn't for my own safety; it was the same thought any father would have in the same circumstance.

"Where's Jordan?"

"Where's my son?"

He hadn't come down to the command bunker. Instead, he was outside, waiting, while I finished my meeting. From the moment the siren sounded until the moment the rocket hit, he had fourteen seconds to get to safety.

Those were the longest fourteen seconds of my life.

The rocket arced high into the air over Gaza. The Hamas rockets were less powerful back then, but the Iron Dome system that protects Israeli civilians today did not exist.

In other words, that rocket wasn't going to be shot down. It was going to land, somewhere close to us. Somewhere close to Jordan.

It hit seventy-five yards from my son. By the grace of God, the angle of the impact combined with the shape of the charge drove the blast away from Jordan. He was unharmed.

But for a few terrifying seconds, I lived the reality of Israeli fathers and mothers—someone was trying to kill my child.

Not just trying, but exerting maximum possible effort.

Hamas has sworn not just to destroy Israel, the world's only Jewish nation, but to kill Jews, to slaughter them. Its intentions mirror those of Hitler, even if its forces are not yet capable of the same kind of destruction.

That is life in southern Israel in the shadow of Hamas, a terrorist organization that digs tunnels with openings near homes and schools. The tunnels are designed to allow squads of terrorists to run out, kill, or capture sleeping families, and dash back to Gaza before even the most rapid-reacting and elite soldiers of the Israel Defense Forces can respond.

Hamas kidnaps and murders children, sends suicide bombers to restaurants, and summarily executes anyone it believes has ties to Israel.

Hamas hides its rockets and bombs in schools and mosques, builds tunnels under United Nations facilities, and often surrounds its fighters with children and other civilians, using them as human shields. It hopes that Israel will either refrain from firing on known terrorists or that, if Israel does fire, enough children will die for the world to express outrage against Israel. In other words, this organization launches rockets hoping to kill children, and when Israel responds, it does all it can to make sure that only Palestinian children die.

Either way, the goal is to kill the most innocent and vulnerable.

Hamas has sworn not just to destroy Israel, the world's only Jewish nation, but to kill Jews, to slaughter them. Its intentions mirror those of Hitler, even if its forces are not yet capable of the same kind of destruction.

It seeks arms from Iran (as Iran is busy building a nuclear bomb), it backs jihadists in Syria, and it is—bizarrely enough—cast as a heroic freedom fighter by millions of Europeans and even a distressing number of Americans.

The goal of this book is simple: to understand the horrific jihadist threat to Christians and Jews in the Middle East, a threat that will undoubtedly come to the United States if it is left unchecked abroad. Through ISIS and Hamas, Christians and Jews face a wave of persecution and violence that is, quite simply, genocidal in scope and intent. But the situation—while grave—is not hopeless. Unlike in dark times before, America actually has strong allies on the ground, willing to take the fight to the jihadists. Even Israel isn't as alone as it has been, with Egypt proving to be even more helpful at times than the Obama administration. In other words, the means exist to stop genocide—if only we have the will to use them.

Let's begin with ISIS. As of the writing of this book, the terrorists of ISIS—once known as al-Qaeda in Iraq—control territory as large as an entire nation-state, with much of northern Syria and northern Iraq under its control. It is threatening Baghdad and the Kurdish capital city of Erbil, and it recently controlled (and still threatens) a poorly constructed dam near Mosul (one of Iraq's largest cities). If that dam is blown, it would drown an entire region in a wall of water, killing hundreds of thousands.

ISIS is brutal beyond imagination to anyone—Christian, Jew, Yazidi, and even Shiite Muslim—who is not aligned with its jihadist form of Sunni Islam. In Syria, ISIS has slaughtered Shiites, Christians, and Alawites (an obscure Islamic sect). In Iraq, it has done the same, giving Christians in conquered territories a chilling ultimatum: "Convert, leave your homes, or die."

Tens of thousands of Christians have fled. ISIS fighters have marked their homes and businesses in much the same way that Nazis marked the Jews of Germany and occupied lands, using an Arabic symbol that has come to mean "Nazarene"—a pejorative Middle Eastern term for Christians. They have sold Christian women as sex slaves, and there are numerous reports that they've beheaded children. None of this is a surprise. All of this is completely consistent with their behavior in Iraq when America previously fought them.

By late 2008, jihadists in Iraq were largely defeated, their leaders killed or captured, along with tens of thousands of their terrorist foot soldiers. Many had fled into Syria, and Iraq became a more stable and more humane place to live than it was when America invaded in 2003.

But now, only six years later, ISIS is stronger than any jihadist group in world history. Americans have long—and rightly—feared al-Qaeda. After all, it carried out the most devastating attack ever on American soil. But if we have feared and fought al-Qaeda, consider the following facts about ISIS:

- ISIS is more brutal than al-Qaeda, so brutal that al-Qaeda tried to persuade ISIS to change its tactics.[1]
- ISIS is the "world's richest terrorist group."[2]
- ISIS controls more firepower and territory than any jihadist organization in history.[3]

- ISIS has reportedly seized "40kg of radioactive uranium in Iraq," raising fears that it could construct a "dirty bomb" that could spread deadly radiation in the atmosphere, rendering entire areas uninhabitable and killing or sickening everyone within the radius of its radiation cloud.[4]

And as if that weren't enough, ISIS's leader, Abu Bakr al-Baghdadi, reportedly told his American captors as he was released (we briefly detained him during the Iraq War), "I'll see you guys in New York."[5] And now an ISIS spokesman has pledged to raise the black flag of jihad over the White House.[6]

ISIS is not the only radical terrorist group in the Middle East. While al-Qaeda still has a presence, Hezbollah threatens Israel in the north, and myriad other terrorist groups fight in Syria, Yemen, Lebanon, and elsewhere. But the one terrorist organization that is making a concerted, daily effort to kill as many Jews as possible is Hamas, the rulers of the Gaza Strip.

Why focus on ISIS and Hamas? Aren't they separate organizations fighting separate enemies? After all, Hamas—a designated terrorist organization under U.S. law—focuses its efforts on Israel while ISIS is fighting virtually everyone *except* Israel. It has launched attacks (moving from west to east) in Lebanon, Syria, and Iraq, and its fighters are now turning up in Iran.

But it is a mistake to think of these groups as entirely separate. Indeed, they are motivated by the same hate, the same faith, and employ many of the same tactics. But they share something else in common, something strategically significant: they do not want to just spread terror; they want to establish terror-run nation-states, permanent bases from which to wage unrelenting jihad.[7]

In fact, the organizations are so similar in goals and tactics that one has only to look to the Christians of Iraq to see what would happen to the Jews of Israel if Hamas were ever to gain the upper hand in its war against Israel. The only difference between the experience of the Christians of Iraq and the Jews of Israel is that the Jews of Israel have the F-16s and tanks of the Israel Defense Forces (IDF) to protect them, while the Christians of Iraq are largely defenseless.

Yes, the Peshmerga militia in Kurdistan has done its best to defend Kurdistan (where tens of thousands of Christians have fled), but it has not been able to stand against the armored vehicles and artillery that ISIS captured from the Iraqi Army. Further, the small and limited American air strikes that defend Iraq pale in comparison to the Israeli bombardment of Gaza that helps protect Israel from Hamas.

In other words, without the means of self-defense, the Christians of Iraq and the Middle East may well be slaughtered. Without their self-defense, the people of Israel certainly would be.

When jihad is on the march, only overwhelming force can stop it.

And that brings us to the next great challenge described in the book, the struggle against the jihadists' allies in the U.N., Europe, and elsewhere—people who would argue that Israel and America must not be allowed to effectively fight jihad.

The U.N. and its leftist friends watch Hamas use human shields and blame Israel when civilians die.

The U.N. and its leftist friends discover that Hamas has been hiding rockets in U.N. facilities, and then applaud as U.N. officials hand those rockets back to Hamas.

The U.N. and its leftist friends watch as Hamas uses its facilities as bases for terror tunnels and then booby-traps U.N. facilities to kill Israeli soldiers, and find no fault.

The U.N. appoints obviously biased "scholars" to investigate alleged Israeli "war crimes," and the international left uses the results of that biased investigation to deprive Israel of its most basic right of self-defense.

And lest you think this campaign to demonize and restrict Israel applies only to our closest Middle East ally and friend—and not to American forces—think again. By attacking Israel, the U.N. and the international left are trying to establish an entirely new "law of war" that would be used to try to tie America's hands as it fights terror at home and abroad. These new rules and regulations would be used to brand our own soldiers as war criminals.

After all, when it comes to our own military tactics in the war against jihadist terrorists, our own military is far less restrained than Israel's.

How do we know? One of my coauthors helped make key decisions in Iraq on when to drop bombs, fire artillery shells, or launch rockets. We know our American rules and practices, and we know Israeli rules and practices, and the Israelis are even *more* constrained than America.

Before they strike, the Israelis will often call or send text messages to warn citizens to evacuate. Before we strike, we give no warnings. Our drone strikes and air strikes come by surprise, deliberately designed to catch as many of the enemy in one place as possible.

And that's our right, under the law of war. But if the international left has its way, we will lose that right. Israel will lose that right. And jihadist terrorists will be left free to fight as savagely as they please—immune from prosecution for war crimes by an indifferent, even sympathetic world.

In the aftermath of the Holocaust, the world vowed, "Never again." Never again would the great powers sit on their hands while an entire people faced extinction. The world has since failed in that pledge, failing to protect the Cambodians from the killing fields, failing to protect the Tutsis of Rwanda even when minimal force could have stopped the killing of hundreds of thousands, and now we're largely watching—once again—as genocide unfolds before our eyes.

But if the international left has its way, we will lose that right. Israel will lose that right. And jihadist terrorists will be left free to fight as savagely as they please—immune from prosecution for war crimes by an indifferent, even sympathetic world.

In the chapters that follow, you will first learn about ISIS—where it came from, its goals, and its capabilities. Then you will learn the same about Hamas, as well as the history of its war against Israel. You will learn about the law of war and war crimes, including who is guilty and who is innocent. You will hear stories about the incredible bravery of men and women in uniform who have confronted the horrors of jihad and laid down their lives to protect the innocent.

Finally, you'll learn what you can do—what our nation can do—to stop an emerging genocide, defeat jihad, and protect Israel. This book is not long, but you'll notice that it is full of footnotes to our sources. In other words, we've done our homework. When you read, you'll be equipped to raise this issue at home, on social media, in our communities, and when you speak or write to your elected representatives. Ignorance is the enemy not just of our democratic system but also of our moral integrity as a nation, as the land of the free and home of the brave. Read this book and you will be informed.

Earlier in this chapter, I described the shock of hearing the siren warning of a rocket attack in Israel. Treat this book as your own siren, as your warning that jihad is on the march.

It has been thirteen years since September 11, 2001, when al-Qaeda (a less brutal organization than ISIS) flew passenger jets into the Pentagon and World Trade Center and hijacked Flight 93 before courageous Americans fought back, causing the plane to crash before its target. Nearly three thousand Americans died. Since September 11, thousands more Americans have died fighting jihad overseas, with tens of thousands wounded.

After all that loss, after all that expense, jihad is still spreading. Indeed, our own government threw away victory in Iraq and is on the verge of leaving Afghanistan to its fate. It is understandable if Americans are weary of thinking about war, of worrying about war. But enemies do not fight on our timetables.

Now is not the time to grow weary in the face of evil. Now is not the time to allow our hunger for peace to obscure our enemy's desire for war. Innocent lives are at stake, and immense evil is on the march. Let's call our nation to action again.

If Americans are war-weary, think about the Israelis. They've likely not had a year without combat since modern Israel was founded in 1948 and was immediately attacked by Arab armies bent on destroying the new nation and driving the Jews into the sea. To be an Israeli means being willing to fight for your life against jihad.

Now is not the time to grow weary in the face of evil. Now is not the time to allow our hunger for peace to obscure our enemy's desire for war. Innocent lives are at stake, and immense evil is on the march. Let's call our nation to action again, before Christians and Jews are slaughtered in the Middle East and before the smoke and flames of terror fill American skies once more.

CHAPTER TWO

THE RISE OF ISIS AND THE NEW CALIPHATE

A sk any combat veteran of the Iraq War—any veteran who spent serious time "outside the wire" (outside the American bases)—about our enemy there, and the stories will flow. In one small region in one year alone, jihadists in Iraq committed the following atrocities:

- Packed explosives in a small boy's backpack (without his knowledge) and detonated the backpack while he was wearing it at a family wedding;
- Put explosives inside the tubing of a child's bicycle and detonated it after the child rode it to a local market;
- Shot a seven-week-old baby in the face, in front of the baby's mother, as a "warning" against collaborating with American forces;
- Raped women and then told them the only way to redeem their honor was to blow themselves up as suicide bombers;
- Used those female suicide bombers (who wouldn't be

stopped and frisked because of cultural and religious pro-
hibitions against male police officers touching women) to
blow up restaurants, hospitals, and open-air markets;

- Faked surrenders inside mosques and then used the cover
of the mosque to ambush American soldiers;

- Put bombs on handicapped children, knowing that American soldiers showed particular compassion for mentally
handicapped or physically impaired kids; and

- Killed entire villages for the crime of resisting Sharia law
or allegedly cooperating with the Iraqi government.

That's a partial list.

And the crimes didn't stop with murder. When AQI—the
forerunner to ISIS—took over a region, it would implement
the most draconian Sharia law imaginable, requiring women
to cover themselves from head to toe, prohibiting most forms
of education for women, and even regulating the kinds of
foods women were permitted to purchase. The repression was
so intolerable, so violent, that even as far back as 2007 and the
increase in U.S. troops in Iraq known as the Surge, the rift
between AQI and al-Qaeda headquarters in Pakistan emerged.
Yet AQI persisted, convinced that its killing spree would usher
in the new Caliphate, a new government.

This new Caliphate is crucial to ISIS. Here's why: Islam
purports to be a universal religion. In other words, its teachings encompass all aspects of life and its ultimate goal is the
establishment of a global Islamic state.[1] This political idea of
Islam is embodied in the concept of the *ummah* (community),
which is the idea that all Muslims, wherever they reside, are

bound together through a common faith that transcends all geographical, political, or national boundaries.[2] This common bond is formed through Muslims' allegiance to Allah and to the Prophet Muhammad.[3] Because Muslims believe that Allah revealed all laws concerning religious and secular matters through the Prophet Muhammad, the entire *ummah* is governed by the divine law, or Sharia.[4] Sharia is applicable at all times and places and, therefore, transcends geographical boundaries and supersedes all other laws.[5]

Traditionally, Islam divides the world into two spheres: the house of Islam (*dar-al-Islam*) and the house of war (*dar-al-harb*).[6] The house of Islam includes nations and territories that are under the control of Muslims and where Sharia law is the highest authority.[7] The house of war includes nations and territories that are under the control of non-Muslims and that do not submit to Sharia.[8] Consequently, under the jihadist interpretation of Islam, there will be constant conflict between the house of Islam and the house of war until the house of war is transformed into the house of Islam.[9] The conflict will not end until all land is conquered for Allah,[10] thereby establishing a single, global, Islamic State, also known as the Caliphate.[11]

The Caliphate is envisioned to be a unified, transnational government ruling over the entire Muslim Community, *ummah*.[12] It is to be governed pursuant to Sharia and enforced by a supreme leader, the caliph.[13] Because Allah alone is the lawgiver, there is no place for a legislator; in Islam, human government exists only to enforce Allah's law.[14]

The caliph's position is to administer and enforce the divine law.[15] The caliph is seen as the "vicegerent of Allah upon earth, charged with the duty of judging righteously, i.e., of applying [Sharia], between men."[16] Accordingly, the "caliphate is the highest type of political organization on earth" and its subjects can derive their highest welfare through "absolute obedience to its ordinances."[17]

Going back to the founding of the Muslim faith, Muslims believed that Allah had delegated to the Prophet Muhammad authority to rule the people with justice.[18] Yet, when Muhammad died, he had neither designated a successor nor provided guidance regarding how to choose a successor.[19] The lack of explicit guidance on how to determine Muhammad's successor has been a prime source of the long-standing, bloody divide between Sunni and Shia Muslims.[20] Shias believe that the caliph must come from the bloodline of the Prophet Muhammad, whereas Sunnis maintain that any believer may qualify for the office of caliph, regardless of his lineage.[21]

The Sunnis had three caliphs before Ali (Muhammad's son-in-law and cousin), who became the fourth caliph.[22] Contending that Ali was the first legitimate successor, Shias dispute the first three Sunni caliphs.[23] Most Shias "consider belief in Muhammad's designation of Ali as his successor a religious duty alongside belief in the oneness of God."[24] Shias therefore believe that the imam, which is the Shia version of the caliph, must be a descendant of Ali.[25] Most Shias are "twelver Shia," who believe that there were twelve imams. The last one is supposed to come back as "Mahdi."[26] (In fact, a number of Shia leaders have claimed to be the Mahdi over the past ten centuries, igniting multiple bloody conflicts, including the Mahdist War against the Egyptians and British in the late nineteenth century.) "Until the Mahdi returns many Shia[s] believe that there will be just ayatollas (a more recent designation) and other levels of Shia scholars in hawzas (scholarly systems) to help explain the religion."[27]

Beginning with the first Caliphate, the caliph would select a place to base the empire.[28] And while the Shias looked for the Mahdi, the Sunnis were busy establishing their own caliphs, including Caliphates ruled from Damascus, Baghdad, and Istanbul.[29] The last Sunni Caliphate was ruled by Ottoman sultans for five hundred years, during the Ottoman Empire.[30]

When the Ottoman Empire collapsed following World War I (the Ottoman Empire sided with Germany in the war, against Great Britain and France),[31] the titles of sultan and caliph were rendered mere names with no real power.[32] "On November 1, 1922, under the leadership of Mustafa Kemal (who later took the name of Atatürk), the newly formed Turkish Grand National Assembly abolished the sultanate, and the last sultan, Murad VI Vahdeddin, fled from Istanbul aboard a British battleship."[33] Atatürk ultimately persuaded the Turkish Assembly to abolish the Caliphate, which it did on March 24, 1924.[34] Abolition of the Caliphate removed a significant symbol of universal Islamic authority, a symbol many Sunni groups wish to restore.

Reestablishment of the Caliphate has been a long-standing goal of Sunni Muslims.[35] The Muslim Brotherhood, for example, was founded in Egypt in 1928 with the goal of reestablishing the traditional Caliphate.[36] Al-Qaeda, ISIS, and other jihadist groups also seek to reestablish a new Caliphate.[37] ISIS has gone further than any other to make that radical dream a present reality.

The new Caliphate in Iraq and Syria is not the first Caliphate proclaimed by jihadists. In 2007, they tried to launch a Caliphate in Diyala Province, Iraq. Calling their new "nation" the Islamic State of Iraq, AQI controlled a vast section of the province and maintained that control until they were finally crushed in 2008.

Why bring this up? Why speak of years past?

Because America has seen this enemy. We have fought this enemy. And we know it can be defeated.

On July 4, 2014, Abu Bakr al-Baghdadi, newly proclaimed "Caliph Ibrahim" and leader of the so-called Islamic State (also known as ISIS[38] or ISIL[39]), delivered a sermon at the Grand Mosque in Mosul, Iraq. In his sermon, al-Baghdadi claimed the mantle of caliph—Allah's vicegerent on earth—and called on fellow Muslims to obey him as they would Allah and Muhammad. Here is the key section of his sermon. It makes for chilling reading:

> Verily your brothers the Mujahidin, Allah Blessed and High be He, has favored them with victory and conquest. And he established for them after long years of jihad and patience, and meeting in combat with the enemies of Allah, he granted them success, empowered them in order to fulfill their purpose. *Verily they hastened to announce the Caliphate and appointing* [sic] *a leader*, and this is an obligation upon Muslims. An obligation which has been made lost for centuries and was absent upon earth's existence, and so many Muslims were ignorant of it. And those who commit sin; where Muslims are

sinning by abandoning and neglecting it, *for verily they have to always strive to establish it and **here now they have established it,** praise and favor is due to Allah.

Verily I am in a trial by this great matter. I am in trial by this trust, a heavy-weighted trust. ***And so I was put in authority over you,*** and I am not the best of you nor am I better than you. If you see me upon truth, then support me; and if you see me upon falsehood, then advise me and guide me and obey me as long as I obey Allah in you. Verily if I disobey Him, then obey me not. I am not to promise you as how the kings and rulers promise their followers and their citizens from luxury, prosperity, security and wealth; but instead, I promise you by what Allah, Blessed and High be He, has promised His believing servants: Allah has promised those who have believed among you and done righteous deeds that He will surely grant them succession upon the earth just as He granted it to those before them. Just as He granted it to those before them and that He will surely substitute for them, after their fear, security, they worship Me, not associating anything with Me. But whoever disbelieves after that—then those are the defiantly disobedient.[40] (Emphasis added.)

Who is this man? Who is making such grandiose proclamations, using the language of a crazed, self-proclaimed prophet?

"Caliph Ibrahim" was born Abu Du'a in 1971.[41] His most recent nom de guerre (many jihadists take on a "war name" to build their legend and strike fear in the hearts of their enemies) is Abu Bakr al-Baghdadi. He grew up in "a religious family in Samarra. . . . He studied Islamic history as a student and . . . gained a doctorate from Baghdad University in the late 1990s."[42] In other words, like many jihadists, he was hardly the desperate, poverty-stricken warrior that the media imagines. "It is likely al-Baghdadi held a religious position in the Sunni community when the United States invaded Iraq in 2003."[43] Following the U.S. invasion of Iraq, al-Baghdadi joined the armed resistance to coalition troops in Iraq, but he was captured and detained in a U.S.-run Iraqi prison in 2006.[44] Following al-Baghdadi's release in the late 2000s, he joined the predecessor to ISIS, the Islamic State of Iraq (ISI).[45] In 2010, al-Baghdadi became the leader of ISI.[46] He changed the name of the organization to ISIS in 2013.

While al-Baghdadi began his terrorist career in Iraq, he truly prospered in Syria. By the end of the Surge, AQI/ISI was largely a spent force, unable to inflict casualties on Americans or Iraqis. The numbers tell the story. For example, in late 2007 in Diyala Province (the heart of the Islamic State of Iraq), 25 percent of all American convoys came under some kind of armed attack. In other words, every time an American soldier rolled out of the gate, he faced a 1-in-4 chance of an IED strike, ambush, or other kind of attack. By the end of 2008, that chance had dropped to 1 in 100. Fewer than 1 percent of all convoys faced combat.

And those improvements were nationwide. For American soldiers, the height of the Surge—2007—was the bloodiest year of the war, with 961 soldiers lost. In 2008, that number shrank to 322, then 150 the next year, 60 the next, and 54 in 2011, the final year of significant American combat operations. Civilian casualties faced a similar sharp drop. From July 2006 to August 2007, no fewer than 1,006 Iraqi civilians died every month, with the casualties peaking in the dreadful month of September 2006, when 3,389 Iraqi civilians died. But by the end of July 2011, when America was ending its involvement, the number had dropped to 121.[47] In other words, jihadists no longer had the power to threaten the Iraqi nation.

These gains happened primarily through sheer force of American courage and will. In my coauthor's area of operations alone, the stories of heroism were legion:

There was the sergeant first-class who helped rescue a convoy from an ambush despite being shot in the neck, refusing medical evacuation until we was certain that every other American casualty was on their way.

There was story after story of young soldiers, seriously injured, who literally fought back at medics who tried to hold them down and take them out of the fight—they were that determined not to leave their brothers behind on the battlefield.

There was the sergeant who literally wrestled two terrorists to the ground with his bare hands, saving his platoon leader from a surprise attack.

Then there were the stories of these same warriors showing kindness to impoverished Iraqis, in one instance, literally braving hostile gunfire to deliver sheep to a community that had lost everything due to the constant combat.

The stories could go on, but it's vital to understand that a dry recitation of numbers does not do justice to the courage of

Americans who fought in Iraq and turned the tide. Many paid the ultimate price, and their sacrifice must be remembered.

In the spring of 2011, however, just as the Iraq War seemed to be winding down, a rebellion broke out in Syria against Bashar al-Assad, the country's brutal Ba'athist dictator (Iraq's Saddam Hussein was also a Ba'athist, a socialist Arab nationalist party that arose in the immediate aftermath of World War II). As the rebellion gained strength, Sunni jihadists—like the remnants of AQI/ISI—flowed into Syria, eager to take another chance to establish a true Islamic state.

And they succeeded.

Facing a corrupt dictator's army rather than courageous and well-equipped American soldiers, jihadists soon dominated the battlefield in much of northern Syria, ruling entire cities and regions. It was in this fight that al-Baghdadi distinguished himself as a skilled battlefield commander and tactician.[48] His battle tactics and leadership skills appealed to young jihadists, to the extent that ISIS may now hold greater appeal for young jihadists than al-Qaeda.[49]

Moreover, under al-Baghdadi's leadership, ISIS prospered financially. ISIS previously relied on donations from wealthy individuals in the Gulf Arab states who were supporting ISIS in the Syrian conflict[50] (donations to terrorists are not unusual in the Muslim world; Saudi Arabia once held a telethon to fund the families of Palestinian suicide bombers). But ISIS now has cash and assets of its own. Al-Baghdadi has secured two primary revenue streams: oil sales from ISIS-controlled oil fields in Syria and sales of antiquities from looted historical sites.[51] ISIS accumulated cash and assets worth an estimated

$2 billion, making it arguably the wealthiest terror organization in the world.[52] When ISIS overran Mosul, Iraq, its forces looted banks of cash and precious metals.[53]

Flush with new-found wealth and empowered by his military success, on June 29, 2014, al-Baghdadi declared himself to be "Caliph Ibrahim."[54] A statement published by ISIS to support al-Baghdadi's designation as caliph listed his qualifications as follows: "The mujahid, the scholar who practices what he preaches, the worshipper, the leader, the warrior, the reviver, the descendant from the family of the Prophet, the slave of Allah."[55]

CHAPTER THREE

ISIS

THE WORLD'S MOST RUTHLESS AND POWERFUL JIHADIST ARMY

ISIS has emerged as not just the most ruthless of the Sunni jihadist organizations in Iraq and Syria; it is also the most successful. ISIS is so extreme that other well-known, radical Islamist and jihadist groups have not only distanced themselves from ISIS, they have also publicly condemned ISIS's actions and even fought ISIS fighters directly.[1] ISIS jihadists commit violence against fellow Muslims in violation of Islamic law; they routinely commit war crimes and engage in torture in violation of international law; and they also kill and threaten Christian, Jewish, and other religious communities. In short, ISIS is composed of religiously motivated psychopaths.

Not only are ISIS leaders and fighters ruthless, but they also have obtained sufficient material assets to support a standing military force. They possess the will to use weapons of mass destruction to carry out their fanatical aims. They're no longer a terrorist gang, but a terrorist army possessing greater striking power than any terrorist force in the Middle East, greater striking power than al-Qaeda ever possessed.

Ominously, this terrorist army is proving to be irresistibly attractive to a subset of British and American Muslim men, with hundreds (if not thousands) flocking to the black flag of jihad. By some estimates up to three hundred Americans currently fight for ISIS, all of them now enemy combatants against their own country. Britain faces an even worse crisis, with more of its Muslim young men volunteering to fight for ISIS than volunteering to serve in their own country's armed forces.

But because the world is full of apologists for Islamic terror, it's critical to enumerate ISIS's crimes, including its crimes against Muslim law. After all, the fight against jihadist terror requires Muslim allies. One key to turning the tide against AQI during the Surge was persuading mass numbers of Sunni men to take up arms against terror, including some to change sides in the fight. These "Sons of Iraq," part of the so-called Sunni Awakening, left the jihadists with nowhere to hide, allowing American soldiers to find and fight the enemy where it lived.

Similarly, in the battle against Hamas, Egypt has emerged as a key Israeli ally, far more helpful in the most recent fight against Hamas than the United States has been.

Why? Because the people of Egypt have a recent and bitter experience with Muslim Brotherhood rule, when Mohammed Morsi and a Brotherhood government initially replaced the Mubarak regime. Elected by a popular majority, the Brotherhood soon wore out its welcome, persecuting Egypt's Christians, taking steps toward implementing Sharia, and providing assistance to terrorists while violating Egypt's decades-old peace treaty with Israel. Egyptians responded with protests so vast that some called them the largest political protests in history, quickly deposing Morsi.

Consequently, the new Egyptian government, fully aware of the threat from the Muslim Brotherhood, rendered invaluable assistance to Israel, shutting down smuggling tunnels into the Gaza Strip and helping choke off Hamas's access to key supplies.

The lesson? There is tremendous value in enlisting Muslim allies against jihad, allies like the Peshmerga in Kurdistan. At the same time, however, we must take great care in selecting those allies. While the Peshmerga have proven themselves, many of the so-called "moderate" Muslim rebels in Syria are nearly as bad as ISIS. In fact, there are now reports that these "moderates" may have kidnapped and sold American journalist Steven Sotloff to ISIS to be beheaded. Some of these "moderates" actively cooperate with al-Qaeda and ISIS. We cannot and must not render the slightest aid and comfort to radical jihadists, no matter how "moderate" the American diplomatic elite claims them to be. Too many Americans have already died at the hands of "moderates." We cannot be held captive to our own wishful thinking.

Still, the Muslim world must know the truth about ISIS. It must see that its strength (which is sadly attractive to many young Muslim men) comes about only through systematic violation of the very Muslim laws it claims to uphold, creating a world that is unbearably violent and oppressive for the citizens of jihadist-held territory.

Claiming to uphold Allah's law, ISIS, in fact, routinely violates Sharia for its own purposes. Sharia law, for example, forbids a Muslim from killing another Muslim unless specific conditions are met. The Quran clearly states that "[i]f a man kills a Believer [Muslim] intentionally, his recompense is Hell, to abide therein (forever): and the wrath and the curse of Allah are upon him, and a dreadful penalty is prepared for him."[2] It also states that a Muslim may not take "life, which Allah hath made sacred, except by way of justice and law."[3]

Ahmad ibn Naqib al-Misri, in *Reliance of the Traveller* (a manual of Sunni Sharia law), quotes a hadith (a record of Muhammad's traditions or sayings) that states:

> The blood of a Muslim man who testifies that there is no god but Allah and that I am the Messenger of Allah is not lawful to shed unless he be one of three: a married adulterer, someone killed in retaliation for killing another, or someone who abandons his religion and the Muslim community.[4]

Other pertinent hadiths are as follows:

> "The killing of a believer [Muslim] is more heinous in Allah's sight than doing away with all of this world."[5]
> "The Prophet said, 'A Muslim is the one who avoids harming Muslims with his tongue and hands.'"[6]

"Some people asked Allah's Apostle, 'Whose Islam is the best? (i.e., Who is a very good Muslim?)' He replied, 'One who avoids harming the Muslims with his tongue and hands.'"[7]

"The Prophet said, 'Abusing a Muslim is Fusuq (an evil doing) and killing him is Kufr (disbelief).'"[8]

ISIS routinely kills its foes, *Muslims and non-Muslims alike*, even when they have not taken up arms against ISIS or have not acted on behalf of any other group—and even when they are disarmed or wounded and wholly at ISIS's mercy. Such killings not only constitute violations of Islamic law and morality; as we will discuss, they constitute war crimes.

But before we get into the details of ISIS's violations of the laws of war and its war crimes, it is important to establish the general principles of the International Law of Armed Conflict. While the precise parameters of the law of war can be complex in any given situation, the law itself is governed by a few relatively simple principles.

First, all combatants must comply with the requirement of *necessity*. In other words, combatants are required to attack only those targets that are necessary to achieve a military objective.

Second, all combatants must comply with the requirement of *distinction*. This principle not only requires soldiers (and

---

While the precise parameters of the law of war can be complex in any given situation, the law itself is governed by a few relatively simple principles.

even jihadists) to distinguish between military and civilian targets when they strike; it also requires them to *distinguish themselves* from civilians. Soldiers wear uniforms not just for the camouflage value or other tactical values, but because the uniforms separate them from civilians. When jihadists fail to wear uniforms or other distinctive clothing that allows enemies to target them separately from civilians, they violate the law of war.

Critically, when combatants violate the principle of distinction, they can convert a civilian target into a military target. So when jihadists use hospitals as command posts, launch rockets from mosques, or store weapons in U.N. facilities, they are converting each of those otherwise-protected civilian structures into legitimate *military* targets under the law of war.

Third, all combatants must comply with the requirement of *proportionality*. This is perhaps the most misunderstood legal principle in the law of war. It does not require, for example, the American military to fight terrorists only with the same weapons that terrorists use. We can respond to sniper fire or RPGs with air strikes. Instead it requires combatants to use the military force necessary to accomplish the military objective, but no more force beyond that. So, if a sniper is in a building, we can drop on that building but not intentionally demolish the entire city block.

Finally, when combatants are captured or incapacitated by wounds, there is a requirement of humane treatment. While the precise requirements for treatment vary depending on the captive's status (prisoner of war or unlawful combatant), torture is always prohibited. At the very least, prisoners are entitled to basic medical care, shelter, and nutrition.

ISIS violates every single principle of the law of war.

ISIS routinely tortures its enemies in violation of international law. ISIS operates a number of detention facilities within its territory, which it uses to punish those who break Sharia law or oppose ISIS. Many of the prisons are clandestine, and few are known. Known detention centers in al-Raqqa, Syria, for example, include: the government building, Mabna al-Mohafaza; the Governor's Palace, Qasr al-Mohafez; a former Ministry of Transport building, Idarat al-Markabat; and a parking garage, al-Mer'ab.[9] A U-shaped building in Sadd al-Ba'ath, which was built in the late 1980s on the Euphrates River, exists as another known detention center.[10] Others include an al-Akershi oil facility twelve miles east of al-Raqqa, a children's hospital in the Qadi Askar area, and Maqar Ahmed Qaddour in the al-Haidariya area.[11]

ISIS violates every single principle of the law of war.

Individuals suspected of violating Sharia law or opposing ISIS, including children as young as eight years old, are abducted and transported to prisons where they are flogged, tortured, and summarily executed.[12] Other targets for abduction and imprisonment include: members of the media, local council members, members of rival rebel groups, members of international organizations, and foreign religious figures.[13]

Reports from former detainees describe various modes of torture common in ISIS prisons: beating detainees with "generator belts, thick pieces of cable, sticks or other implements"[14] and forcing detainees to remain in "contorted stress position[s] . . . for long periods, inducing severe pain and possible long-term muscular or other damage."[15] One detainee reports being "tortured with electric shocks and beaten with a cable while suspended with only one foot touching the floor."[16] Other detainees claimed that ISIS utilizes solitary confinement[17] and electric shocks.[18] Still other reports indicate that ISIS members flog early-teenage prisoners with anywhere from 30 to 94 lashes at a time.[19]

(As with all other ISIS tactics, this is nothing new. AQI maintained "torture houses" in territory it controlled, and our soldiers routinely uncovered the most gruesome scenes imaginable. The ones detailed below are only a portion of what can be described.)

ISIS routinely targets civilians and military prisoners (like Syrian or Iraqi soldiers) and executes summary justice against civilians and soldiers in the most brutal, inhumane ways possible. ISIS's most recent wave of violent, public executions began in March 2014 when ISIS accused a shepherd of murder and theft and summarily executed him by shooting him in the head.[20] In a grotesque, symbolic display of authority, ISIS fighters tied the lifeless body to a cross and displayed it in the public square.[21] Again, in May 2014, ISIS publicly executed seven men in al-Raqqa, Syria, hanging two of the bodies on crosses and leaving them there for more than three days.[22] A bystander who witnessed the killings claimed that the other five bodies were not displayed because the victims were all "children under the age of 18, one of them a seventh-grade student."[23] On May 29, 2014, militants from ISIS executed at least fifteen civilians in northern Syria by shooting them in the head or chest.[24] Residents said that at least six children were among those killed.[25]

Since ISIS's surge back into Iraq, the group has escalated its violent shows of force. On June 15, 2014, ISIS released video footage of five unarmed Iraqi soldiers being taunted and forced to praise ISIS before being summarily shot.[26] The ISIS soldier responsible for the execution then filmed himself saying, "Praise to Allah, whether he is a believer or not, I killed him. I killed a Shia! I killed a Shia!"[27] On that same day, ISIS used social media to spread photographs and videos depicting massacres at seven different sites in Iraq.[28] An analysis done by Human Rights Watch concluded that, in two mass graves near Tikrit, Iraq, ISIS left the bodies of between 160 and 190 men it had executed.[29]

ISIS has increasingly utilized decapitation to carry out its public executions, though it has also carried out executions in private and disseminated the execution videos through social media.[30] For instance, on June 13, 2014, ISIS posted a picture of a decapitated head on Twitter, along with the following text: "This is our football, it's made of skin #WorldCup."[31] By using the "WorldCup" hashtag, ISIS managed to expose the gruesome photograph to thousands of unsuspecting Twitter users who were simply following the FIFA World Cup on the social networking site.[32] The law of war flatly prohibits the desecration of human remains.[33]

Throughout mid-June 2014, ISIS carried out numerous executions in Iraq. Witnesses have testified that ISIS shot dozens of soldiers and policemen, concluding their gruesome killings by decapitating their victims and placing rows of decapitated heads along the road in Mosul.[34] A refugee woman said that placing decapitated heads in a row has become "a trademark, trophy-style execution favored by ISIS militants."[35]

On June 16, 2014, ISIS reportedly captured Judge Raouf Abdul Rahman, the judge who sentenced Saddam Hussein to death in 2006.[36] Although the Iraqi government did not confirm it at the time, it is believed that Judge Rahman was executed by ISIS militants two days after his capture in apparent retaliation for his role in Hussein's death.[37]

Simply put, ISIS attacks moderate Sunni Muslims, Shia Muslims, and Christians wherever it finds them. For example, when ISIS was asked why it was "not fighting Israel but instead shedding the blood of the sons of Iraq and Syria,"[38] it replied as follows:

> The greater answer is in the noble Koran, when Allah Almighty speaks about the near enemy. In the majority of verses in the noble Koran, these are the hypocrites, for they pose a greater danger than the original infidels [born non-Muslims, e.g., Jews and Christians]. And the answer is found in Abu Bakr al-Sadiq, when he preferred fighting apostates over the conquest of Jerusalem [*fath al-Quds*], which was conquered by his successor, Omar al-Khattab.[39]

ISIS also cited the example of Saladin, who dealt with Shias before the Crusaders:

The answer is found in Salah ad-Din al-Ayubi [Saladin] and Nur ad-Din Zanki when they fought the Shia in Egypt and Syria before [addressing] Jerusalem. Salah ad-Din fought more than 50 battles before he reached Jerusalem. And it was said to Salah ad-Din al-Ayubi: "You fight the Shia and the Fatimids in Egypt and allow the Latin Crusaders to occupy Jerusalem?" And he responded: "I will not fight the Crusaders while my back is exposed to the Shia."[40]

As ISIS has moved into areas with larger Christian populations, it has continued and even escalated its brutal tactics. "Islamist insurgents have issued an ultimatum to northern Iraq's dwindling Christian population to convert to Islam, pay a religious levy, or face death."[41] ISIS set Saturday, July 19, 2014, as the deadline for Christians to decide.[42] Nearly fifty thousand Christians have also been displaced from Qaraqosh, a town twelve miles east of Mosul.[43] The Christians were displaced because their water and electricity were cut off from neighboring ISIS-controlled Mosul.[44] Christians were not the only ones affected by the attack: Yazidis, Shias, and liberal Muslims were also displaced from the region.[45] ISIS views all four of these groups as "infidels without human rights."[46]

Christians were not the only ones affected by the attack: Yazidis, Shias, and liberal Muslims were also displaced from the region.[47] ISIS views all four of these groups as "infidels without human rights."[48]

As Christians and Yazidis fled, ISIS pursued, trapping tens of thousands of Yazidis on a mountaintop and threatening horrific mass murder until the siege was lifted by emergency American air strikes. ISIS pursued Christians to the outskirts of the Kurdish capital, Erbil, where thousands had fled for refuge. The Peshmerga, brave but hopelessly outgunned by ISIS forces equipped with captured American-made weapons, were forced to retreat. Kurdistan faced a disaster until, once again, American air strikes temporarily halted ISIS advances.

But ISIS is not content with spreading jihad in Iraq and Syria. It has set its sights on much larger targets. For example, ISIS has threatened to destroy the Kaaba in the Grand Mosque in Mecca, Saudi Arabia.[49] A tweet reportedly posted by an ISIS fighter stated: "If Allah wills, we will kill those who worship stones in Mecca and destroy the Kaaba. People go to Mecca to touch the stones, not for Allah."[50] This is consistent with ISIS's practice of destroying shrines, tombs, mosques, and other religious sites in territory controlled by ISIS.[51] ISIS believes that giving veneration to tombs or religious relics violates Islamic teachings.[52] ISIS routinely threatens other Muslims who disagree with them, most notably Shia Muslims.[53]

On June 25, 2014, ISIS began a campaign to threaten America by using social media to post warnings and pictures of executed victims, using the hashtag "#CalamityWillBefallUS."[54] ISIS circulated a picture of "a dozen armed masked-men standing around a body" while one ISIS fighter held the decapitated head of a Shia fighter.[55] Tweets accompanied by the #CalamityWillBefallUS stated: "We will kill your people and transform America to a river of blood :)!"; "EACH and

EVERY #American is targeted, whether he lives in or outside the #US!"; "THIS SCENE WILL BE SEEN BY #AMERICANS BUT WHERE? UNEXPECTED PLACE" (accompanied with a picture of the 9/11 World Trade Center terrorist attack); and "Every American doctor working in any country will be slaughtered if America attack [*sic*] Iraq" on a picture.[56]

ISIS's hatred of America is long-standing. After all, American forces not only brought ISIS to the brink of extinction in 2008 and 2009, but we captured and held its current leader, al-Baghdadi. Upon his release from American custody, he ominously told his former captors, "I'll see you guys in New York."

ISIS fighters have also declared their intention to destroy Israel and to make Jerusalem the capital of the new Caliphate.[57] ISIS militants and ISIS media have threatened Israel on multiple occasions. A July 9, 2014, tweet by an ISIS media wing posted a picture of the Dome of the Rock superimposed in front of a picture of ISIS fighters with the words, "Patience, Jews, our appointment is at al-Quds [Jerusalem] tomorrow."[58] Another ISIS Twitter feed stated: "All our military operations till now are just [a] message for Israel."[59] Even before its recent territorial gains, ISIS maps regularly included Israel as a part of the eventual Caliphate.[60] A recent video posted by ISIS states, "[w]herever our war goes, Jewish rabbis are humiliated," and "[b]reak the crosses and destroy the lineage of the grandsons of monkeys," undoubtedly references to Christians and Jews.[61] ISIS threats against Israel are not new. In 2008, al-Baghdadi proposed to use Iraq as a launching pad for missile attacks against Israel.[62]

In a video posted in early July 2014, two Spanish-speaking men stated that Spain is the land of their forefathers and that they are willing to die for the newly established Islamic State.[63] One of the men stated, "We are going to die for it until we liberate all the occupied lands, from Jakarta to Andalusia."[64] Further, in an audio recording posted online, al-Baghdadi states:

> So to arms, to arms, soldiers of Islam, fight, fight. Rush O Muslims to your state. It is your state. Syria is not for Syrians and Iraq is not for Iraqis. The land is for the Muslims, all Muslims. This is my advice to you. If you hold to it you will conquer Rome and own the world, if Allah wills.[65]

This statement is a direct threat to the historical center of the Catholic Church.[66]

Grandiose threats are nothing new in the jihadist world, but what makes ISIS *especially* dangerous is its possession of both the means and will to carry out its threats. It's the best-equipped, richest terrorist force in the world.

ISIS has a huge war chest of money, military equipment, and materials available to carry out its threats. ISIS has captured significant amounts of high-tech U.S. military equipment

---

Grandiose threats are nothing new in the jihadist world, but what makes ISIS *especially* dangerous is its possession of both the means and will to carry out its threats. It's the best-equipped, richest terrorist force in the world.

abandoned by the Iraqi armed forces. Fifty-two 155 mm M198 howitzers have been captured by ISIS.[67] These American-made howitzers have a range of up to twenty miles and can incorporate GPS targeting systems.[68] In addition to the howitzers, ISIS has captured 1,500 Humvees and 4,000 PKC machine guns that can fire close to 800 rounds per minute.[69] These weapons make ISIS a formidable foe in the region. There are even reports that ISIS has captured main battle tanks, including potentially several M1 Abrams tanks, the American-made tank that is the most lethal armored vehicle in world history.[70]

Ominously, ISIS also possesses radiological material that could make dirty bombs. Dirty bombs are created by combining conventional explosives with low-level radioactive material.[71] If a dirty bomb is detonated, in addition to the raw blast effect of the bomb, it can spread radiation in a wide area, potentially causing radiation sickness to those exposed and rendering the area uninhabitable for an extended time.

ISIS has stolen eighty-eight pounds of uranium compounds from Mosul University and has the capacity to gain even more radioactive material.[72] Waste recovered from universities and hospitals across northern Iraq has the potential to contribute radioactive material for a dirty bomb.[73] Further, it is not beyond imagination that ISIS could also obtain chemical weapons from Syrian depots for its arsenal. In fact, it has already captured old stocks of Iraqi chemical weapons.[74] Were ISIS to obtain increasing amounts of weapons of mass destruction, the global danger of this group would increase exponentially.

But this book focuses on more than just ISIS. While there

is not sufficient time and space to outline the threat of every jihadist group in every corner of the Muslim world, from Yemen to Lebanon, Nigeria to Mali, Libya (where al-Qaeda-affiliated terrorists carried out the deadly Benghazi attacks on September 11, 2012) to Pakistan and Afghanistan, there is one other group that is not only vicious and deadly, but is engaged in constant, open warfare against our closest ally in the Middle East, Israel.

That group is Hamas.

CHAPTER FOUR

HAMAS
ARCHITECTS OF ETERNAL JIHAD

Our battle with the Jews is long and dangerous, requiring all dedicated efforts. It is a phase which must be followed by succeeding phases, a battalion which must be supported by battalion after battalion of the divided Arab and Islamic world until the enemy is overcome, and the victory of Allah descends.

—Hamas Charter, Preamble

It would be hard to find an American who hasn't at least seen a Sbarro restaurant. How many times have we walked on city streets or through an airport or mall and passed by a Sbarro, glancing at it without a thought as kids and families indulge their insatiable hunger for a good slice of pizza?

On August 9, 2001, families and kids at a Sbarro in Jerusalem were doing exactly what families and kids love to do in America: eat pizza. School was out, so the restaurant was packed with teenagers. The atmosphere was festive.

Until 2 p.m.

That's when a Hamas suicide bomber walked in, either wearing a suicide belt or carrying explosives in a guitar case. Regardless of where he kept his bomb, it was packed—like most suicide bombs are—with nails, bolts, and other small metal scraps, all designed to tear human flesh and maximize human agony.

He self-detonated.

When the smoke cleared, fifteen people lay dead—including seven children and one pregnant woman. One hundred thirty more were wounded, some with horrific injuries.

Initially, Hamas denied responsibility, incredibly blaming Israel for murdering its own children. But it later praised the bomber, honoring him as a man who "gave the Zionists a taste of humiliation."[1]

This suicide bombing was hardly unusual for Hamas. In the so-called Second Intifada, Hamas carried out suicide bombing after suicide bombing, invariably targeting Israeli civilians—killing as many as it could, as often as it could. After much hard fighting, Israel defeated Hamas in the West Bank. But it was relatively unscathed in the Gaza Strip, where it consolidated control until it ruled the entire area with an iron grip, launching thousands of rockets at Israeli civilians.

Its crimes are easy enough to chronicle, but who is Hamas? Why is it so relentless in its quest to kill Jews? A bit of history is necessary.

The two principal Palestinian groups representing the Arabs of Palestine are Fatah,[2] the political arm of the Palestine Liberation Organization (PLO),[3] and Hamas,[4] the Islamic Resistance Movement,[5] an offshoot of the Muslim Brotherhood.[6] As of the last free Palestinian presidential election,[7] Fatah's candidate for president, Mahmoud Abbas, was elected president of the Palestinian Authority (PA),[8] while Hamas candidates won a majority of the legislative seats in the 2006 parliamentary election.[9] As a result, for the last several years, Fatah and Hamas have been competitors whose respective followers have attacked each other.[10] In fact, in 2007, Hamas assumed total control in the Gaza Strip and has held total power there ever since.[11] Moreover, while Fatah has publicly renounced resorting to violence in pursuit of an agreement with Israel,[12] Hamas has refused to do so. In fact, the Hamas Charter declares violence to be a legitimate means to use against Israel.[13]

The Hamas Charter declares violence to be a legitimate means to use against Israel.[14]

The United States, Canada, and the European Union have all declared Hamas to be a terrorist organization.[15]

Hamas "is one of the wings of the Muslim Brotherhood."[16] It was established on the eve of the intifada (also known as the "First Intifada")[17] in December 1987 by Sheikh Ahmed Yassin and Mahmoud Zahar with one specific purpose—to eliminate Israel and return all of Palestine to Islamic control, "rais[ing] the banner of Allah over every inch of Palestine."[18] Sheikh Yassin, a Muslim Brotherhood activist in Cairo, was a spiritual leader who founded the Islamic Center (al-Mujamma' al-Islami) in 1973 "to coordinate the Brotherhood's political activities in Gaza."[19] In December 1987, Yassin founded

Hamas "as the Brotherhood's local political arm."[20] Shortly after its founding, the group published its covenant (also called the Hamas Charter) in 1988, stating its purpose in chilling detail.

The Hamas Charter opens with verses from the Quran, proclaiming the superiority of Islam,[21] with Hamas's stated motto in Articles 5 and 8: "Allah is its goal, the Prophet its model to be followed, the Koran its constitution, Jihad its way, and death for the sake of Allah its loftiest desire."[22] The Charter proclaims: "Israel will exist, and will continue to exist, *until Islam abolishes it*."[23] The entire Hamas Charter, from its preamble to the last article, pursues only one purpose: the violent elimination of Israel.

The Charter proclaims that "Palestine is an Islamic land. In it is the first of the two *qiblas* [directions of prayer] and the third most holy mosque, after the mosques of Mecca and Medina. It is the destination of the Prophet's nocturnal journey."[24] Further, consistent with Sharia law, the Charter states that

[T]he land of Palestine is *Waqf* land given as endowment for all generations of Muslims until the Day of Resurrection. One should not neglect it or [even] a part of it, nor should one relinquish it or [even] a part of it. . . . This is the legal status of the land of Palestine according to Islamic law. In this respect, it is like any other land that the Muslims have conquered by force, because the Muslims consecrated it at the time of the conquest as religious endowment for all generations of

Muslims until the Day of Resurrection. . . . This *Waqf* will exist as long as the heaven and earth exist. Any measure which does not conform to this Islamic law regarding Palestine is null and void.[25]

Accordingly, the Hamas Charter calls the existence of the state of Israel on the land that was formerly held by Muslims a "Zionist invasion."[26] It therefore pledges to wage *"jihad* in the face of the oppressors, in order to deliver the land and the believers from their filth, impurity, and evil"[27] in order to "[return the homeland to its rightful owner] and "to raise the banner of Allah over every inch of Palestine"[28] no matter how long it takes.[29]

Hamas does not want "peace" with Israel, and it will not negotiate a permanent peace agreement with Israel. Instead, it will only agree to intermittent "truces" when its military capabilities have been so degraded that it needs time to recuperate and rearm.

Its Charter states that "so-called peace solutions" and "conferences are nothing but a way to give the infidels power of arbitration over Muslim land."[30] The Charter declares that "[t]here is no solution to the Palestinian problem except by *jihad.*"[31] As reflected in Hamas's Charter and actions, *jihad* here does

---

Hamas does not want "peace" with Israel, and it will not negotiate a permanent peace agreement with Israel. Instead, it will only agree to intermittent "truces" when its military capabilities have been so degraded that it needs time to recuperate and rearm.

---

not mean spiritual struggle. In the preamble, Hamas commits to "join arms with all those who wage *jihad* for the liberation of Palestine."[32] It states, "our fight with the Jews is very extensive and very grave, and it requires all the sincere efforts.... [B]rigades upon brigades from this vast Islamic world [must be reinforced], until the enemies are defeated and Allah's victory is revealed."[33] The Charter declares that "neglect[ing] any part of Palestine [means] neglect[ing] part of the Islamic faith."[34]

Accordingly, from its inception, Hamas has relentlessly waged jihad and attacked Israel in accordance with its stated purpose and Islamic teachings.[35] Through its military wing, the Izz al-Din al-Qassem Brigades, Hamas has conducted numerous suicide bombings, rocket attacks, and shootings against Israeli targets.[36]

Western entities, including the United States, the European Union, and Canada, have declared Hamas to be a terrorist organization.[37] The United States officially designated Hamas as a Foreign Terrorist Organization on October 8, 1997.[38] On December 21, 2001, the European Union adopted a measure to combat terrorism that listed Hamas's military wing, Izz al-Din al-Qassem, among its recognized terrorist groups.[39] In 2003, the European Union designated Hamas's political wing as a terrorist group.[40]

Despite Hamas's terrorist reputation, it maintains significant popular support because of its involvement in a "broad network of 'Dawa' or ministry activities."[41] Hamas donates a significant portion "of its estimated $70 million annual budget" to social establishments as varied as food banks, schools, medical clinics, and sports leagues.[42] According to Israeli scholar Reuven Paz, "approximately 90 percent of its work is in social, welfare, cultural, and educational activities."[43] Hamas uses these social programs to spread its doctrine of hatred toward Israel, for example by publishing textbooks that refuse to recognize Israel's existence and by calling "Zionism a racist movement" bent on driving Islam from the Middle East.[44]

Despite Hamas's terrorist reputation, it maintains significant popular support because of its involvement in a "broad network of 'Dawa' or ministry activities."[45]

There are signs, however, that Hamas's eternal quest to kill Jews is diluting its commitment to placate Gaza's citizens through its "ministry activities." The discovery of an extensive network of terror tunnels reaching from Gaza into Israel (sometimes with exit points close to Israeli homes and schools) demonstrates that Hamas has in fact been diverting an enormous share of its budget to terror activities—up to 40 percent.[46] This has included diverting even international aid into building its terrorist infrastructure.

In contrast with Hamas, Fatah is a secular group that was founded by Yasser Arafat and a small group of Palestinian nationalists in the late 1950s.[47] Its existence and purpose were a secular version of Hamas's quest to destroy Israel, based on the ideas that "the Palestinian Arab people possess the legal right to their homeland" and that "armed struggle is the only way to liberate Palestine."[48] In 1969, Arafat became chairman of the PLO's executive committee, an event that transformed Fatah from "a resistance group [in]to a legitimate political party and the largest faction within the PLO."[49]

For decades, the PLO led the Palestinian fight to "liberate" Palestine from the "Zionist invasion"[50] (in plain English, it meant the PLO was trying to destroy Israel entirely, not co-exist with a Jewish state). Yet, once it determined that the military option was not succeeding (after decades of war), the PLO in 1993 recognized Israel's right to exist in pursuit of a two-state solution with Israel.[51] Hamas, however, has adamantly refused to follow the PLO in recognizing Israel and has vowed to continue the "resistance."[52] Hamas has even chastened the PLO in its charter:

> Owing to the circumstances that surrounded the establishment of the PLO . . . the PLO has adopted the idea of the secular state. . . . Secularist ideology stands in total contradiction to the religious ideology, and it is ideas which are the basis of positions, behavior and decisions. Hence, with all our appreciation for the Palestine Liberation Organization and what it may yet become, and without belittling its role in the Arab-Israeli conflict, we cannot give up the Islamic identity of Palestine in the present and in the future to adopt the secularist ideology—for the Islamic identity of Palestine is part of our faith, and whoever is lax with his faith is lost.[53]

Following unsuccessful peace talks with Israel and Arafat's death in 2004, a rift developed between the PLO's "old guard" of Arafat confidants and the "new guard," members of the next generation who sought to gain leadership positions for themselves.[54] As Fatah experienced internal strife, Hamas defeated Fatah in the 2006 parliamentary election and took control of the Gaza Strip the following year.[55] Hamas has treated Fatah members with the same kind of savage disregard for human life seen in ISIS's conduct in Syria and Iraq, killing Fatah members through summary executions, even tossing some from the tops of tall buildings in Gaza.

Despite this history of conflict, Fatah and Hamas in recent years have engaged in periodic efforts to form a unified Palestinian government. Their hope is that the political unity would benefit both parties and possibly result in the fringe benefit of having Egypt open its border for the passage of fuel and other necessities into Gaza.[56] But these reconciliation efforts have had absolutely no effect on Hamas's conduct. In fact, since the latest round of "unity" talks and unity agreements, Hamas has stepped up attacks against Israel, ultimately triggering another major confrontation.

CHAPTER FIVE

HAMAS

ISRAEL'S MOST RELENTLESS ENEMY

Since Hamas was established in December 1987, it has opposed any political compromise with Israel and has continued to attack Israel with suicide bombings and rockets. In fact, there has not been a year since its founding that Hamas has been at peace with Israel, or even contemplated peace. Hamas typically attacks Israel through its military wing, the Izz al-Din al-Qassem Brigades. Their attacks against Israelis in Gaza continued steadily until 2005. That is when Israel pulled out of the Gaza Strip as part of an effort to create a "two-state" solution to the Israeli-Palestinian conflict in the absence of a permanent peace agreement.[1]

In fact, there has not been a year since its founding that Hamas has been at peace with Israel, or even contemplated peace.

After Hamas took over Gaza in 2006, the Brigades "transformed from an underground guerrilla organization into a uniformed military force designed to protect Gaza from outside attack."[2] In 2009, the International Crisis Group[3] estimated the Brigades had between 7,000 and 10,000 full-time members, with more than 20,000 members in reserve.[4] However, rather than protect Gaza from outside attack, Hamas's main military tactic since taking over Gaza "has been an increased firing of rockets and mortars from the territory" into Israel.[5] These rocket attacks have frequently landed in Israel's border towns, resulting in occasional deaths and less serious injuries. In reality, if Hamas were not attacking Israel, Gaza would not be suffering from "outside attack." Israel only strikes Gaza in

---

Israel has said it would actively work to build Gaza's infrastructure and economy if Hamas would repudiate violence.

---

self-defense, when rockets are fired, and has often expressed that it has no territorial designs on Gaza. In fact, Israel has said it would actively work to build Gaza's infrastructure and economy if Hamas would repudiate violence.

Hamas refuses.

It is estimated that Hamas killed more than four hundred Israelis between 1993 and 2010.[6] Although such attacks have been separated by periods of temporary calm, Palestinian terrorist groups have persisted in launching rockets into Israel, often in spite of cease-fire agreements.[7] Israel has recognized that groups other than Hamas have participated in the attacks, but Israeli prime minister Benjamin Netanyahu has stated that, because Hamas exercises full control of Gaza, "Israel holds Hamas responsible for all the attacks launched on [Israel]."[8] The worst of Hamas's attacks include the following:[9]

- Rocket barrages: The IDF claims that terrorists in the Gaza Strip (including, but not limited to, Hamas) have fired more than "8,000 rockets into Israel, killing 44 Israelis and injuring more than 1,600" from 2005 to 2011."[10]
- Suicide bombings: During a nine-day span in February and March 1996, Hamas carried out four separate suicide bombings that killed 61 Israeli citizens and injured 234 others.[11]
- Mass-casualty suicide attacks: One of the deadliest attacks was on March 27, 2002, when a suicide bomber entered the dining room of the Park Hotel in Natanya, Israel, and detonated his explosives amid 227 guests who were eating their Seder meal. The Passover attack killed 30 Israelis and left 143 wounded.[12]
- Coordinated suicide attacks: In 2003, Hamas suicide bombers attacked three separate buses, killing 56 and wounding more than 240, many of them students and children.[13]

Yet despite its unquestioned terrorist identity, Hamas seeks and often obtains recognition and funding from the Western powers.

No reasonable person can conclude that Hamas is anything but a vicious terrorist organization, restrained from mass murder only by the power of the Israel Defense Forces. Yet despite its unquestioned terrorist identity, Hamas seeks and often obtains recognition and funding from the Western powers.

CHAPTER SIX

HAMAS CREATES A UNITY GOVERNMENT WITH FATAH, THEN LAUNCHES WAR

In June 2014, Hamas and Fatah announced they were forming a unity government.[1] This means the secular Fatah was joining with the jihadist Hamas to attempt to govern the Palestinian territories together, under the banner of the Palestinian Authority (PA). The Obama administration, within days of this announcement, pledged that the United States would continue to provide hundreds of millions of American taxpayer dollars in aid to this new terrorist government.[2] The administration is pledging this aid despite the fact that U.S. criminal law clearly prohibits any material support for designated terrorist organizations like Hamas.[3]

Currently, the operating relationship of this new unity government is unclear. The Palestinian Authority is a larger entity with a primary role in the Israeli-Palestinian peace process, while Fatah is a more moderate political organization and Hamas is a terrorist gang.[4] To draw a crude and imperfect analogy with the United States, our nation is governed by a federal government, which is—depending on the year—controlled by either the Democrats or Republicans (and sometimes control is divided). The Palestinian Authority, by contrast, has long been controlled by Fatah, with Hamas largely excluded from the PA. With the creation of the unity government, however, Hamas may now have a say in PA governance not unlike that of an American political party in governing the United States. It is not yet known what duties are delegated to which organization, how future endeavors will be orchestrated, or how the Palestinian people can trust that their goals will be pursued effectively.

What is clear, however, is this new unity agreement has not moderated Hamas, which followed the announcement of the unity government by dramatically escalating its terrorist attacks against Israel.

Hamas orchestrated the kidnapping and brutal execution of three teenagers in June 2014.[5] These teenagers were shot ten times with a silenced gun.[6] As follows many terrorist atrocities, the kidnapping resulted in Palestinian celebrations at a university near Ramallah.[7] Palestinians were seen giving away sweets and celebrating in the streets.[8]

Hamas did not disclaim responsibility. Far from it. The military branch of Hamas issued a statement that said "the occupier will never have security," without mentioning the three kidnapped teens.[9] Hamas followed the kidnappings by stepping up its rocket launches into Israeli territory, firing them indiscriminately at Israeli civilians.[10] Although the majority of these rockets have thankfully fallen on unoccupied ground or have been intercepted by the Israelis' Iron Dome antimissile system,[11] they are nonetheless being fired at civilians in violation of the law of war.[12] In response to these rockets, Israel acted in self-defense by conducting air strikes and raids with ground troops against Hamas and other terrorist operatives in Hamas-controlled Gaza.[13]

Israel simply cannot negotiate with Palestinian officials who refuse to acknowledge or accept Israel's right to exist, and who continue to support or mount attacks on Israel.

In the final analysis, until Hamas and its terrorist allies are defeated, there will be no peace with Israel. There will be continued terrorist attacks directed against Israeli civilians, attacks that violate the international law of war and constitute war crimes. The Palestinian people will be pawns in the hands of vicious terrorists and will continue to suffer the inevitable results that Hamas's terrorist attacks invite on their own neighborhoods and families.

In the final analysis, until Hamas and its terrorist allies are defeated, there will be no peace with Israel. There will be continued terrorist attacks directed against Israeli civilians, attacks that violate the international law of war and constitute war crimes. The Palestinian people will be pawns in the hands of vicious terrorists and will continue to suffer the inevitable results that Hamas's terrorist attacks invite on their own neighborhoods and families.

The only thing that separates the Jews of Israel from the fate of the Christians, Yazidis, and other religious minorities in Iraq and Syria is the might of the Israel Defense Forces. Faced with murderous terrorists, Israelis are able to respond with F-16s, Merkava tanks, and one of the best-trained armies in the world. In Iraq, by contrast, Christians are defenseless, Yazidis are helpless, and even America's Muslim allies, the Kurds, are outgunned by their barbaric ISIS enemies. Tragically, our friends in Iraq are defenseless because America chose to abandon them. American air strikes designed to avert world-historic massacres may be too little and too late to preserve any semblance of Christian life in Iraq.

If self-defense is all that separates Israel from defeat and genocide—if self-defense is all that prevents jihadists from killing American allies and striking America again and again—then the U.N. and our Western allies should support the rights of Israel and America.

But they often do not. Western European governments, in cooperation with the U.N. and the international left, systematically seek to prevent Israel from defending itself, and use legal arguments that would also apply to American soldiers.

And this brings us to the next troubling phase of our battle against jihad, our battle to save Israel, America, and Christians in the Middle East from destruction and death—the legal battle to preserve America's and Israel's right to protect themselves.

The battle against "lawfare."

CHAPTER SEVEN

WAGING LAWFARE

THE U.N. TRIES TO TRANSFORM OUR SOLDIERS INTO WAR CRIMINALS

The mission of AQI (the forerunner of ISIS) was to kill anyone it could. In my coauthor's area of operations, the terrorist group was in the habit of launching mortar shells in the general vicinity of American soldiers, but instead of hitting our bases, the shells kept hitting in and around local villages. Our soldiers had been hunting for the mortar crew for days, but without success. The mortar was kept in the back of a pickup truck. The terrorists would race out to a firing point, fire two or three deadly shells, then race back under cover before anyone could see them.

While their fire had not yet claimed any American lives, the Iraqi civilians were not so lucky. AQI fired at American bases, around American bases, and sometimes directly into Iraqi villages, even when no Americans were within miles.

Finally, on one very hot afternoon in July, our soldiers got lucky. Very lucky. The terrorists had pressed their luck in daylight, rushing out to a firing point next to a small stand of trees in the bleak Diyala countryside. They did not see or hear the American Apache helicopter hovering two miles away.

When AQI fired, the Apache crew saw the puff of smoke from the mortar, then the impact near an Iraqi village, and immediately swung to attack. As the helicopter approached, ready to fire its cannon and destroy the mortar truck, the terrorists heard the "thump" of the rotors, jumped out of the truck, and ran away.

There were four men.

Three went one way, one went the other. The Apache directed nearby American ground troops to intercept the group of three while it tracked the lone runner with its gun camera. He was running straight into a village, ducking under the shade of houses, sprinting as fast as his legs could carry him.

But he was running out of room. In mere moments he would run out of the village and into the open desert, where the Apache would get a clear shot.

At the last possible moment, just before the Apache pulled the trigger to end the terrorist's life, he did what so many of them did.

He grabbed a human shield.

He scooped up a small child, cupping a young boy in his left arm like a football, and kept running.

Could the American crew fire? If they did and the child was hurt, who would be legally responsible for the child's death?

Under the law of war, there was no doubt the terrorist was a war criminal. He violated multiple provisions of the law of war. His indiscriminate mortar fire was only occasionally aimed at military targets, so he violated the rule of *necessity*. His attacks were not necessary to accomplish legitimate military objectives.

By dressing like a civilian and firing at civilian and military targets alike, he was doubly guilty of violating the rule of *distinction*. He did not distinguish between military and civilian targets, and through his civilian clothes he tried to blend in with civilians as much as possible, increasing the risk that American return fire would inadvertently hurt the innocent.

Then, by scooping up the child, he not only engaged in hostage taking, but immediately mistreated his captive by intentionally placing that child in mortal danger.

Moreover, as a war criminal, he was legally responsible for all the harm that resulted from his crimes, not only the deaths that may have resulted from his mortar attacks, but the deaths that resulted when American forces used their right of self-defense. In other words, if American forces fired and the child died, the terrorist would be legally responsible for the child's death.

So, yes, we had the right to fire. The war criminal was the terrorist, not the Apache aircrew.

But the Apache crew, like so many Americans before and after them, did not fire. They did not press that trigger. They could not bear to kill a child, and they knew something that the terrorist forgot: the day was very, very hot—125 degrees hot.

And kids are heavy.

So our soldiers waited and watched as he carried the child for almost a full kilometer before collapsing, exhausted, in the open desert. While the Apache hovered over him, American soldiers closed in and captured him. Tragedy was averted.

Talk to virtually any American or Israeli veteran of a combat unit and he can tell you several stories that are remarkably similar. And they usually do not have happy endings. Soldiers ambushed from mosques have to return fire. Terrorist leaders surround themselves with civilians so often that troops face the terrible choice of either allowing terrorists to roam free and execute deadly attacks, or having to kill them and face the reality of civilian deaths.

A terrible and hidden reality of both America's and Israel's wars is that hundreds of soldiers have fallen, killed by terrorists, *because they were being cautious with civilian lives.* This is an impulse that is utterly alien to jihadists, but is a core value for Americans and Israelis. Terrorists take a life for the purpose of taking a life. American and Israeli soldiers take a life in the effort to save civilians.

A terrible and hidden reality of both America's and Israel's wars is that hundreds of soldiers have fallen, killed by terrorists, *because they were being cautious with civilian lives.*

So, why then does the U.N. and much of the international left try to turn American and Israeli soldiers into war criminals? Why do they claim that Americans or Israelis are responsible for civilian deaths when it is the terrorists who strike from schools, hospitals, and mosques, often while using women and children as human shields?

The answer is relatively simple: The U.N. and international

left often want to see terrorists prevail. They want Israel and America to take terrible losses, to withdraw, and to accommodate terrorist demands. So they wage "lawfare."

A good definition of lawfare is the abuse of international law and legal processes to accomplish military objectives that can't be accomplished on the battlefield. Can't beat the IDF? Use the International Criminal Court to tie its hands, restricting its operations until terrorist forces have the upper hand. Can't stop American attacks on al-Qaeda? Use the U.N. to try to declare its drone strikes unlawful, placing America in a terrible bind: either risk boots on the ground or let terrorists plot and plan in safety and security.

At the ACLJ we've confronted this "lawfare" directly. After the 2008 Gaza war (called "Operation Cast Lead"), Palestinian officials attempted to charge Israel with war crimes in the International Criminal Court, a tribunal typically reserved for the worst war criminals in the world. Yet Israel's alleged "crimes" were nothing of the sort. Indeed, Israel's protective measures (including sending text messages or phone calls to civilian areas in danger of air strikes) far exceed even America's.

After a multiyear effort, which included multiple oral interventions at the ICC, we succeeded in persuading the ICC to drop the case. Unfortunately, however, the left never admits defeat. It just tries again.

So Israel once again faces international condemnation and investigation for military tactics that are more conservative than America's. If Israeli soldiers are judged to be war criminals, then so will our own men and women in uniform, and the terrorists will have won a dramatic victory without ever winning a battle.

CHAPTER EIGHT

THE 2014 GAZA WAR
WHO ARE THE REAL WAR CRIMINALS?

As explained previously, Hamas's kidnapping and murder of three Israeli teenagers sparked the latest escalation in the ongoing war between Israel and Hamas.[1] In response to the kidnappings, Israel launched Operation Brother's Keeper in the West Bank, a search-and-rescue mission to find the missing teens.[2] The Israeli investigation identified two Hamas operatives as suspects.[3] While Hamas did not at first claim responsibility for the kidnappings, Hamas officials publicly praised the kidnappings and subsequent murder of the three Israeli teens as "heroic,"[4] in itself a despicable act.

The kidnappings were followed by rocket fire.

On June 28, six rockets were launched from Gaza into Israel.[5] In response, Israel struck twelve targets in Gaza on June 29.[6] On June 30, the bodies of the three Israeli teens were found.[7] Following the discovery of the slain Israeli teens, a Hamas spokesman warned that if Israeli prime minister Netanyahu "brings a war on Gaza, the gates of hell will open to him."[8] On July 1, Israel launched 34 air strikes on Gaza in response to 18 rockets fired at Israel from Gaza.[9] On July 7, Israel Defense Forces announced from its Twitter account the commencement of "Operation Protective Edge in #Gaza against #Hamas, in order to stop the terror #Israel's citizens face on a daily basis."[10]

When it comes to the use of force against or by nation-states, international law is clear: the threat and the use of force against a U.N. member state are prohibited.[11] Thus, every Hamas rocket attack violates international law. Every single one.

Article 51 of the U.N. Charter recognizes "the inherent right of individual or collective self-defense if an armed attack occurs against a Member of the United Nations."[12] It is essential to note that Article 51 does not *create* the right of self-defense; it is an *inherent* right of all states under customary international law.[13] This inherent right of self-defense (and the responsibility for determining when self-defense is appropriate) lies, as it always has, with the government of each state. Customary international law also recognizes the right of self-defense against nonstate actors,[14] like the terrorist group Hamas and its Islamist allies in the Gaza Strip.

Additionally, when one is acting in self-defense, international law "does not require a defender to limit itself to actions that merely repel an attack; *a state may use force in self-defense to remove a continuing threat to future security*."[15] In other words, to use a historical example, when Imperial Japan attacked the United States on December 7, 1941, our right of self-defense was not limited to merely shooting back at the planes attacking

Pearl Harbor but included the right to declare war on Japan and fight its military until it surrendered. Hamas's rocket attacks give Israel the right—should it choose to exercise that right—to destroy Hamas.

In addition, the standard for self-defense does not limit the defender to a totally like-kind response, but provides the necessary flexibility to reduce or eliminate the threat. In other words, the degree of force employed in self-defense can be considerably greater than that used in the original armed attack.[16] So, yes, Israel can respond to rockets with F-16s.

This means that Israel, as a sovereign state, has the inherent right to defend its territory and citizens. It was legally justified in engaging in the 2014 conflict against Hamas, as it has been in every significant clash with Hamas since Hamas was formed. Since the most recent conflict began, Hamas repeatedly refused to accept a number of cease-fire proposals,[17] while Israel consistently honored cease-fire requests to allow humanitarian assistance into Gaza.[18] Hamas breached at least four cease-fires during the conflict.[19] The fourth negotiation resulted in an agreement to have a seventy-two-hour cease-fire. Hamas militants broke the cease-fire a mere ninety minutes after it had begun by attacking and killing Israeli soldiers.[20]

Although more Palestinian civilians died than Israeli civilians, Israel was acting within the law of war while Hamas was not. War crimes are not proved merely by citing casualty statistics but by evaluating and understanding the *reasons* for casualties. Israeli civilian casualties occurred because Hamas was intentionally attacking civilians. Palestinian civilian casualties occurred because Hamas intentionally hid behind civilians and fought from civilian structures. Palestinian civilian casualties occurred *despite* Israel's best efforts to minimize collateral damage.

Article 52 of Additional Protocol I to the Geneva Conventions requires that "attacks shall be limited strictly to military objectives."[21] Military objectives are defined as "those objects which by their nature, location, purpose or use make an *effective* contribution to military action and whose total or partial destruction, capture or neutralization, in the circumstances ruling at the time, offers a *definite* military advantage."[22] Notably, "[t]he presence of a protected person may not be used to render certain points or areas immune from military operations."[23] This means that the use of human shields cannot trump Israel's (or America's) right of self-defense.

Since the beginning of Operation Protective Edge in late summer 2014, many international organizations—including the U.N. and even, sadly, the International Committee of the Red Cross—roundly and publicly condemned Israel's actions for damaging or destroying specific targets. Among such targets have been hospitals, schools, places of worship, and civilian areas that are *normally* protected objects under the law of war. In the Red Cross's own words, however, "[i]n combat areas it often happens that purely civilian buildings or installations are occupied or used by the armed forces and *such objectives may be attacked*, provided that this does not result in excessive losses among the civilian population."[24] Determining whether incidental injury or collateral damage violates the law requires analysis of the military advantage anticipated by striking the relevant military target. Many states, including the United States, judge military advantage in the context of the entire operation, not just an isolated part.[25] The "security of the attacking forces" is also a critical part of the consideration in assessing military advantage (in other words, soldiers don't have to die to avoid civilian casualties).[26] The standard is intended to prevent "[m]anifestly disproportionate collateral damage inflicted in order to achieve operational objectives."[27]

Hamas repeatedly and continually used protected civilian sites for military attacks, rendering them legitimate military targets. An IDF study shows that Hamas fired rockets from amusement parks, first aid stations, U.N. facilities, playgrounds, hospitals, medical clinics, and schools.[28] Consequently, Hamas, not Israel, is the party committing war crimes.

Incidental or collateral damage on both sides may occur during an armed conflict. Such damage, including deaths and injuries of innocent civilians, does not automatically (or necessarily) constitute a war crime. Only "willful killing" or "[i]ntentionally directing attacks against civilian objects, that is, objects which are not military objectives," constitutes a war crime.[29] Civilian casualties alone do not render those attacks unlawful. *Only civilian casualties that are excessive in relation to the importance of the military objective are forbidden.*

It's important to go through Hamas's actions and Israel's response chapter and verse. The left has become all too good at simply reciting lurid casualty statistics, as if that proves Israel's or America's crimes. But in war—as always—facts matter. And as John Adams said, "Facts are stubborn things."

So let's look at the facts.

CHAPTER NINE

HAMAS SYSTEMATICALLY AND INTENTIONALLY VIOLATED THE LAW OF WAR

Each party to a conflict has a duty, "to the extent feasible, to remove civilian persons and objects under its control from the vicinity of military objectives" as set forth in Article 58(a) of Additional Protocol I.[1] Furthermore, "in no event may civilians be used to shield military objectives."[2] In the context of the most recent conflict, both Hamas and Israel were required to do everything feasible to avoid locating military objectives near dense civilian populations[3] and were forbidden to use civilians as human shields.

This obligation is explicitly established by Article 51 of Additional Protocol I and is considered a reflection of customary international law:

The presence or movements of the civilian population or individual civilians shall not be used to render certain points or areas immune from military operations, in particular in attempts to shield military objectives from attacks or to shield, favor or impede military operations. The Parties to the conflict shall not direct the movement of the civilian population or individual civilians in order to attempt to shield military objectives from attacks or to shield military operations.[4]

The prohibition on the use of human shields is reiterated in Article 28 of the Fourth Geneva Convention Relative to the Protection of Civilian Persons in Time of War, which again prohibits the use of civilians "to render certain points or areas immune from military operations."[5] Furthermore, under the Rome Statute, the use of humans to shield a military target constitutes a war crime.[6] Such use of civilians to shield military targets is contrary to the principle of distinction and violates the obligation to take feasible precautions to separate civilians and military objectives.[7]

Article 48 of Additional Protocol I sets forth the following basic rule of distinction—a rule we've discussed repeatedly throughout this book: "In order to ensure respect for and protection of the civilian population and civilian objects, the Parties to the conflict shall at all times distinguish between the civilian population and combatants and between civilian objects and military objectives and accordingly shall direct their operations only against military objectives."[8] The Red Cross recognizes that "the parties [to a conflict] are obliged to take all feasible precautions to spare the civilian population," pointing to the "distinction that must be made between civilians and those directly participating in hostilities" and recognizing that such a distinction lies "at the heart of international humanitarian law."[9]

These rules apply to "each" party to the conflict. Thus, Hamas and Israel are legally obligated to minimize their operations near civilians. While most on the left recognize the reality of this legal mandate, the left—along with the U.N. and the Red Cross—has overwhelmingly criticized Israel for targeting certain sites and objects, and has been silent about Hamas's actions that have turned otherwise protected sites and objects into legitimate military objectives—a violation of the law of war. By so doing, the left, the U.N., and the Red Cross encourage Hamas to continue its illegal tactics by providing it a significant propaganda victory over Israel every time innocent women and children are killed or injured by an Israeli attack on a legitimate military target that Hamas has intentionally located in a civilian area. Every time the left defends Hamas, it provides direct incentives to ensure that more women and children die.

Hamas intentionally rejects its duty to avoid civilian casualties. Hamas militants frequently and indisputably "operate in civilian areas, draw return fire to civilian structures, and on some level benefit in the diplomatic arena from the rising casualties."[10] Hamas has intentionally located its military compounds and weapons caches in or next to civilian houses, mosques, and hospitals.[11] Where is the international condemnation?

Let's look at Hamas's violations in detail.

After all, details matter.

According to Article 16 of Additional Protocol I of the Geneva Convention, places of worship are protected objects.[12] To "use [such objects] in support of the military effort" constitutes a war crime.[13] While the international community has condemned Israel for attacking mosques (not a war crime in itself, unless indiscriminately targeted), the U.N., the Red Cross, and other organizations steadfastly refused to condemn Hamas rocket launches from mosques.

Hamas launched 331 rockets at Israeli civilians from mosques during the most recent Gaza conflict.[14]

But Hamas did more than just launch rockets from mosques. On July 22, 2014, an IDF paratrooper was killed by an anti-tank missile fired from within the Khan Younis mosque.[15] The Red Cross condemned Israel for attacking the Khan Younis area, without mentioning that Hamas had invited such attacks by engaging in military operations there.[16] While Hamas is openly and notoriously committing war crimes, the lack of such information in Red Cross statements encourages Hamas to continue using houses of worship to launch attacks on Israelis.

Schools are also protected sites—protected sites that Hamas regularly uses to launch attacks. Hamas located a rocket launch site near a complex of Gaza City schools.[17] On July 16, the U.N. Relief and Works Agency (UNRWA) discovered twenty rockets hidden in a vacant Gaza school.[18] Using the building as a weapons storage site turned that structure into a legitimate military target. More alarmingly, it has been reported that the rockets discovered by the UNRWA were returned to Hamas by U.N. officials.[19] This not only rewards unlawful behavior but quite literally aids and abets Hamas in its unlawful war against Israel.

Again on July 22, UNRWA found more rockets in a second Gaza school.[20] The school in which the rockets were found in the second incident is located between two other schools that housed 1,500 refugees from the fighting—rendering them literal human shields for Hamas rocket storage facilities.[21] The U.N. secretary-general, Ban Ki Moon, "expresse[d] outrage, and regret, at the placing of weapons in a U.N.-administered school."[22] Secretary-General Moon also acknowledged that the location of weapons in such schools transforms those schools into "military targets."[23] Unfortunately, despite this statement from even a biased U.N., the Red Cross has not condemned Hamas for committing a war crime by using schools for military purposes. Instead, it has criticized Israel for attacking them, which further encourages Hamas to violate the laws of war.

Hamas launched 248 rockets from schools at Israeli civilians during the most recent Gaza conflict.[24]

While Israel expends significant resources on building shelters and antimissile equipment to protect its civilians from rockets fired indiscriminately from the Gaza Strip, Hamas, instead of building shelters to protect the population of Gaza, diverts such resources to build tunnels in civilian areas for military uses,[25] including under mosques, schools, and U.N. facilities. These tunnels were constructed and have been used by Hamas militants to enter and attack Israel.[26] IDF forces have found at least thirty tunnels since the beginning of Operation Protective Edge;[27] ten tunnel openings were found underneath the Shujaiya neighborhood.[28] Moreover, Hamas has fired more than 140 rockets from the Shujaiya neighborhood into Israel.[29]

By placing the entrances to its tunnel network within the densely populated Shujaiya neighborhood and firing rockets from the same area, Hamas intended to use the civilian population as a shield, thereby "render[ing] [the Shujaiya neighborhood] immune from [Israeli] military operations."[30] This is a clear and unambiguous violation of the law of war and constitutes a war crime under the Rome Statute.[31]

Hamas launched 818 rockets at Israeli civilians from general civilian neighborhoods during the most recent Gaza conflict.[32]

Hamas isn't content with firing rockets and launching attacks from mosques, schools, and neighborhoods. It is also well-known for using hospitals as cover for its military operations. Hamas placed a rocket cache next to the Jabaliya Indonesian Hospital.[33] Hamas stored weapons in the Al Wafa Hospital[34] and frequently fired on IDF troops from the hospital with light weapons, antitank missiles, and rockets.[35] Al Wafa Hospital is close enough to the Israeli border that one can view Israel from it.[36] A tunnel opening used by Hamas was located adjacent to the Al Wafa Hospital.[37] As such, Israel determined that Al Wafa Hospital was not being used for its normal protected purpose and was instead being used as a military installation, making it a legitimate military target.[38] An IDF video showing the targeting of the hospital reveals extensive secondary explosions after the initial Israeli air strike, vindicating Israel's position that the hospital was used by Hamas as a weapons storage facility.

Hamas turned the hospitals into legitimate military targets when it conducted military operations from or near them. As such, these "purely civilian buildings [were] occupied [and] used by [Hamas] and such objectives may be attacked."[39]

Hamas launched forty-one rockets at Israeli civilians from hospitals during the most recent Gaza conflict.[40]

As explained earlier, Article 52 of the Additional Protocol I of the Geneva Convention recognizes that "a place of worship, a house or other dwelling or a school," although generally protected, can sometimes be used to make "an effective contribution to military action," and the law of war allows attacking it if such an object makes "an effective contribution to military action and whose total or partial destruction . . . offers a definite military advantage."[41]

Thus, because Hamas uses otherwise protected buildings and facilities to store weapons, to serve as command centers, or as locations from which to fire at Israeli forces, they become legitimate military targets. Such facilities make an "effective" contribution to Hamas's military action and the destruction of which offers a "definite" military advantage to Israel. As such, by converting otherwise protected civilian buildings into legitimate military targets, Hamas violates the law of war.

It's difficult to list in a short chapter all of Hamas's war crimes. Hamas violated the law of war not just in the locations of its weapons but also in the targets it chose. When Hamas launches rockets at civilian areas in the hope that they'll kill someone—anyone—it violates the principles of necessity and distinction with every single rocket launch. They are indiscriminate. Indiscriminate attacks are those that are launched without consideration as to where harm will fall[42]—just *like Hamas rocket attacks into southern Israel*. Indiscriminate attacks are defined as

(a) [T]hose which are not directed at a specific military objective; [and]

(b) [T]hose which employ a method or means of combat which cannot be directed at a specific military objective[.] [43]

Specifically, attacks are indiscriminate if they are "expected to cause incidental loss of civilian life, injury to civilians, damage to civilian objects, or a combination thereof, *which would be excessive in relation to the concrete and direct military advantage anticipated*." [44] When Hamas fires rockets into Israel, not knowing where they will land, there is no "concrete and direct military advantage anticipated," and, hence, such firing violates the law of war.

Hamas fired more than 2,900 rockets into Israel since July 8, 2014, before the end of the most recent conflict.[45] At least 280 rockets that were intended to land in Israel landed inside Gaza instead,[46] meaning that Hamas is killing and injuring its own people. Taking into consideration the inaccuracy of Hamas's rockets alone allows one to conclude that Hamas's rocket attacks are indiscriminate because they are a "means of combat which cannot be directed at a specific military objective."[47] Yet Hamas openly boasts that its rockets "accurately target the homes of the Israelis and the Zionists."[48] As such, *by its own admission*, Hamas's rocket fire is not directed at a "specific military target," but rather at civilian homes, thereby establishing—without question—a war crime. Sadly, the U.N. and Red Cross have not denounced this criminal activity, thereby leaving Israel unprotected by the very governing bodies that guide and restrict Israel's defense maneuvers.

As such, Hamas should be held solely responsible for the vast majority of civilian casualties in the current conflict, and the U.N., Red Cross, and governments across the world should be loudly condemning Hamas's violations. Instead, they criticize Israel. The Obama administration went so far as to call a lawful Israeli strike—a strike similar to those that American forces have made hundreds of times in Iraq, Afghanistan, and elsewhere—appalling and "disgraceful."

That is shameful and despicable. And it objectively aids terrorists.

Hamas's actions violate and mock the principles of the law of war, whereas Israel's actions seek at all times to comply with the spirit and letter of the law. The U.N., the Red Cross, and even—on occasion—the Obama administration have lost their own moral authority and credibility by siding with Hamas and advancing the jihadists' interests and narrative of war.

CHAPTER TEN

THE STAKES COULD NOT BE HIGHER

Let's be crystal clear: If the U.N., Red Cross, and even the Obama administration win the legal argument, nations like Israel and the United States will no longer have a meaningful right to defend themselves. If direct warnings of an attack are insufficient, when can a nation defend itself against jihadists who are violating the laws of war? Such rules would give terrorists (who care nothing for the law) safe havens throughout cities and towns as they appropriate and strike from civilian buildings.

It has never been the law that any fighting force, anywhere, enjoys a safe haven when it strikes its enemies. Jihadists, who systematically violate the laws of war, should be the least protected of all combatants. To provide them with any protection at all merely guarantees that civilians will be placed in the crosshairs again and again.

The international left, the U.N., and the Red Cross understand this reality. They are not fools. One can only conclude that they are objectively siding with brutal war criminals, rendering them complicit (and in the case of the U.N., often explicit co-conspirators) in war crimes.

Let's take the example of the International Red Cross, a formerly respected international organization that loses its moral authority with every pro-Hamas statement. In a recent article, the Red Cross discussed an Israeli strike on a seven-story building in Gaza. In the article, the Red Cross made the following statement:

> The ICRC engages in discussion with "both parties" about the "rules of war." We talk about principles such as "precautions in attack," "legitimate targets," "concrete military advantage" and "proportionality." We remind everybody that if an attack is expected to cause "excessive incidental civilian casualties" in relation to the concrete and direct military advantage anticipated, it must be cancelled or suspended. We say loudly and clearly that in this war, as in any other, it is not acceptable that soldiers minimize their risks at the expense of civilians on the other side. We also say it is not acceptable to use civilians as human shields, in any conflict. We attend diplomatic conferences, we organize workshops, we "raise awareness" among belligerents to "minimize casualties." How effective is all this?[1]

Such statements are both self-serving and misleading—especially when it is clear that one side (Israel) is making herculean attempts to fully comply with the law of war and the other side (Hamas) violates the law as a matter of intentional, premeditated strategy. There is no moral equivalency here. Readily available evidence establishes *beyond doubt* that Hamas is routinely, openly, and notoriously violating the law of war. Yet Israel is singled out by the Red Cross, the U.N., and the Obama administration for actions it would have preferred to avoid altogether, but for the incessant attacks on Israeli soil from Hamas-controlled Gaza. The U.N. is going so far as to launch an investigation of *Israel*, the only party to the conflict that complies with the law of war.[2]

The Red Cross and the U.N. consistently ignore or minimize the fact that Hamas built tunnels in civilian areas or stored weapons in hospitals and schools, or that the Israeli military warns civilians (the very civilians Hamas put in danger in the first place) through various means before attacking a military target. The paragraph quoted above does not state which party in the conflict is violating the "rules of war." While Hamas spends millions of dollars to dig tunnels in civilian areas to attack Israel[3] and puts Palestinian civilians (whom Hamas purports to represent) in the line of fire, Israel builds shelters for its people. While Hamas brags about its use of human shields,[4] Israel makes conscious attempts to abide by the rules of war to protect civilians.

In this book we have taken great pains to explain exactly how groups like Hamas and ISIS systematically violate the law of war in a depraved effort to create maximum human suffering. I would say that we have pulled no punches, graphically describing exactly how evil these enemies are. But though we want the reader to know the truth, the whole truth is simply too much for most people to bear. It is too graphic to print, to describe fully.

Veterans of our wars in Iraq and Afghanistan—as well as the IDF's veterans of conflicts in Gaza and Lebanon—will carry with them sights and experiences they can never forget. These memories will haunt them for a lifetime. They have witnessed evil as great as any the world has ever seen. They have witnessed evil acts from enemies that would re-create Auschwitz and Dachau if they could, from enemies who have openly declared war not just on Israel, but on the Jewish people themselves.

The fact that millions across the world support those enemies over Israel and the United States, even going to great lengths to strengthen terrorists and weaken the IDF and the U.S. military, demonstrates that the spirit of murder and collaboration that haunted much of Europe under Nazi occupation has not disappeared. It has only morphed into the preening high-mindedness of leftist "thought."

History rightly looks at Neville Chamberlain and other appeasers of Hitler's Germany as instruments of death and disaster. Today's appeasers are not morally better and are indeed often much worse. After all, when Chamberlain appeased Hitler, Germany's leader had not yet unleashed his murderous armies across Europe. When the U.N., Red Cross, and—sadly—even our own American president and State Department appease jihad, they do so with eyes wide open, fully aware of the evil they empower.

They should hang their heads in shame.

CHAPTER ELEVEN

OPPOSE, DON'T APPEASE
THE WAY FORWARD AGAINST JIHAD

How many times do we have to learn the same lessons? Evil cannot be appeased, and the effort to do so leads invariably to death and heartbreak.

Don't believe me? Ask the Jewish people.

The history of World War II is by now too well known to repeat. A Europe that was desperate to avoid repeating the horrors of World War I (then known as the Great War and the War to end all Wars) refused to believe that Hitler presented an existential threat to peace and democracy, preferring to believe he could be negotiated with, boxed in, and contained.

Right the historical wrongs, grant him the territorial gains he demanded, and there would be "peace in our time." But instead of the promised peace, there was death on a scale the world had never seen.

And no one suffered more than the Jews.

Fast-forward just a few years to 1948. The world, shocked by the Holocaust, finally facilitated the immigration of an ever-larger number of Jews to their ancestral homeland, Israel. There the Jewish people could carve out their own state, protect themselves from genocide, and—finally—have a land to call home.

But then the world washed its hands of the problem, largely leaving the Jews of Israel to fend for themselves when, just three years after the end of World War II, Arab armies massed to destroy the brand-new Jewish state. As the young Israeli state fought armies equipped with modern weapons with the scraps they could beg for, borrow, and steal, the Arab countries launched a systematic and massive ethnic cleansing of Jews within their borders:

> It is, sadly, a little-known fact that almost a million Jews lived in Arab countries when Israel declared independence in 1948. Now, there are less than 10,000. To take a few examples, 250,000 lived in Morocco, 140,000 in Iraq, 80,000 in Egypt, 140,000 in Algeria, and roughly 50,000 in Yemen. But now? 3,000 in Morocco, 100 in Iraq, 100 in Egypt, none in Algeria, and only a few hundred in Yemen. This [was] ethnic cleansing on a grand scale.[1]

How did this happen? The typical way:

> Jews were shot, homes were burned (sometimes in front of cheering crowds), and governments confiscated their property. Anti-Semitic mobs surged through streets, and the Jews fled, often airlifted to Israel as they left

the homes of their fathers (and their fathers' fathers) behind.[2]

A world weary of war refused to confront jihadists and Arab nationalists who had not yet begun to fight. Only Israel's fierce resolve prevented yet another genocide, a genocide only three years after the Holocaust—only three years after the world promised "never again."

In the United States we thankfully don't have a history of genocide, but we do have a recent history of failed appeasement.

During Bill Clinton's presidency, the Palestinian terrorist Yasser Arafat was invited to spend more time in the White House than any other foreign leader—thirteen invitations.[3] Clinton was dead set on helping the Israelis and Palestinians achieve a lasting peace. He pushed the Israelis to grant ever-greater concessions until the Israelis were willing to grant the Palestinians up to 98 percent of all the territory they requested.

And what was the Palestinian response? They walked away from the bargaining table and launched the wave of suicide bombings and other terrorist attacks known as the Second Intifada.

And what of Osama bin Laden? Even while America was granting concessions to Palestinians—and thereby theoretically easing the conditions that provided much of the pretext for Muslim terror—bin Laden was bombing U.S. embassies in Africa, almost sank the USS *Cole* in Yemen, and was well into the planning stages of the catastrophic attacks of September 11, 2001.

After President George W. Bush ordered U.S. forces to invade Afghanistan and Iraq in 2001 and 2003, respectively, bringing American troops into direct ground combat with jihadists half a world away, many Americans quickly forgot the recent past and blamed American acts of self-defense for "inflaming" jihad.

One of those Americans was Barack Obama.

Soon after his election, Obama traveled to Cairo, Egypt, where he delivered a now-infamous speech that signaled America's massive policy shifts. The United States pulled entirely out of Iraq despite the pleas of "all the major Iraqi parties."[4]

In Egypt, the United States actually backed the Muslim Brotherhood government, going so far as agreeing to give it advanced F-16 fighters and M1 Abrams main battle tanks, even as the Muslim Brotherhood government was violating its peace treaty with Israel and persecuting Egypt's ancient Coptic Christian community. The Obama administration continued supporting the Brotherhood, even when it stood aside and allowed jihadists to storm the American embassy, raising the black flag of jihad over an American diplomatic facility.

In Libya, the United States persuaded its allies to come to the aid of a motley group of rebels, including jihadists. Then many of these same jihadists promptly turned their anger on the United States, attacking our diplomatic compound in Benghazi the afternoon and evening of September 11, 2012—killing the American ambassador and three more brave Americans.

Compounding this disaster, the administration had steadfastly refused to reinforce the American security presence in spite of a deteriorating security situation, afraid that it would anger the local population. This naïve and foolish administration decision cost American lives.

During the most recent conflict between Hamas and Israel, the administration consistently rebuffed both Israel and Egypt, preferring instead to advance proposals that empowered Hamas's most staunch allies—Qatar and Turkey. This action not only undermined Israel but also—ironically enough—undermined Egypt as well as every other Palestinian group that had chosen not to join the latest round of fighting.

In other words, the Obama administration rewarded Hamas for its terrorist violence.

Even when the crisis in Iraq became so grave that tens of thousands of Christians and Yazidis faced imminent massacre, the Obama administration's military response was feeble. It consisted of pinprick attacks combined with a promise that ISIS had nothing to fear over the long run from the United States. The Obama administration emphatically emphasized, "This is not the authorization of a broad-based counterterrorism campaign against [ISIS]."[5]

And as it made these declarations, it still refused to provide our Kurdish allies with the heavy weapons they needed to repel an ISIS invasion.

In other words, the Obama administration rewarded Hamas for its terrorist violence.

Again and again, President Obama appeased jihadists.

In the meantime, the jihadists only grew stronger and more dangerous, contemptuous of the United States.

But when it comes to jihad, America must oppose, not appease.

How can it oppose jihad? Does it necessarily have to engage in indefinite ground combat in the Middle East? Do we confront even more frustrating "nation building"?

At this time, we do not believe large-scale ground combat is necessary to battle the latest wave of jihad. In Iraq, we have willing allies, much stronger allies than we had at the time of the 2003 invasion. And Israel has more than enough military strength to repel attacks on its homeland; it needs only American support to resist crushing international pressure to stand down in the face of jihad, pressure that always allows jihadists to ultimately live to fight another day.

In fact, the Kurds possess the numbers and will to drive ISIS back and inflict severe losses on the jihadists.

First, America must commit to destroying ISIS, not just "managing" it or limiting its influence. To do so, we must support our true allies with arms, equipment, military advisers, and—if necessary—military power. Presently, the Kurds possess the fighters and will to defend Kurdistan and protect the thousands of Christians and others who have sought refuge there. In fact, the Kurds possess the numbers and will to drive ISIS back and inflict severe losses on the jihadists.

They do not, however, possess the weapons they need.

There is no excuse for this failure. There is no excuse for abandoning friends in need. The message we're sending to the Muslim world is intolerable—that the world's largest military power will not lift a finger to protect its friends. Nothing drives recruits to jihadists faster than the idea that they are strong while America and its allies are weak.

It is time for America to make its allies strong and demonstrate that jihadists are weak. It is imperative that jihadists face strong *Muslim* opposition. And it is that very need that makes the Obama administration's reluctance to support proven Muslim allies—like the new Egyptian regime and the Kurds—most puzzling. Yet, at the same time, the administration seems all too willing to support unproven "moderates" in Syria, or even forces that have proven to be nothing but unreliable, hostile jihadists. We don't "win" if we defeat ISIS but only end up empowering the jihadists of Iran or competing Sunni jihadists.

Why abandon our allies while empowering potential enemies? The Obama administration has consistently overestimated its ability to "win over" the Muslim Brotherhood or other jihadist organizations. And in trying to win them over, it harms our true allies again and again. This strategy was misguided from the start, and it is now nothing short of foolish after more than five years of consistent and deadly failure. And if President Obama persists in this folly, Congress must do all that it can to end any American funding for jihad.

Further, when supporting our allies we cannot and must not begin by placing explicit limits on the use of our own military power. We must commit to fight to win, and beginning any military effort by announcing explicit limits on our use of force or announcing explicit limits on the length of our commitment merely provides the enemy with a roadmap to victory. While large-scale ground combat may not be necessary, we cannot lead our enemy to believe that he will never face American troops.

Second, outside of Iraq and Syria, America must send a clear message to the Palestinian Authority: it will not get one dime of American taxpayer money while it has any formal or informal ties with Hamas. America will not support jihad anywhere, including in Palestine. Even further, America will not support any easing of the blockade of Gaza until Hamas is removed from power and the Gaza Strip is demilitarized, and it will fully support Israel's acts of self-defense, including by defending Israel in the U.N. and from any effort by any Western power to impose any kind of economic sanctions or arms embargos on Israel.

Third, America must signal its zero tolerance for jihadists by investigating U.N. ties to terrorists, including the U.N.'s inexcusable actions in Gaza, such as allowing Hamas to store rockets in U.N. buildings, booby-trap U.N. facilities, and build terror tunnels from U.N. structures. It should end any American support or funding for any U.N. or other international entity that collaborates with or aids and abets terror.

Fourth, America must not treat Afghanistan like Iraq and abandon it to jihad. We understand that Americans are weary of war, but our enemies are not. Wars do not end when we grow tired of fighting them. They end when our enemies are defeated.

Americans are weary of war, but our enemies are not. Wars do not end when we grow tired of fighting them. They end when our enemies are defeated.

You will notice a consistent theme in all these points: un-wavering strength. While jihad has flared off and on again throughout Muslim history, that same history tells us that when it is dealt a decisive defeat, it can lie dormant for decades. Jihad thrives on victory, not defeat, and it spreads when it is seen to be strong. Expose its weakness, grind its forces into dust, and the jihadist impulse wanes dramatically.

When confronting the pure evil of jihad, our allies do not need to be just like us. They do, however, need to be allies—capable of defeating our enemies and protecting the most basic human rights of their citizens. We cannot be sidetracked into trying to make everything perfect. Much American blood and treasure has been spilled trying to transform Iraq and Afghanistan into modern democracies. Let's settle for strong allies first, and worry about perfecting political systems later. We can defeat jihad. We've done it before.

In Iraq in 2005 and 2006, the situation in many ways was even more bleak than it is today. The entire nation of Iraq was coming apart at the seams, with combat raging not just in the north but across the length and breadth of the entire nation. Shiite militias ruled in the south, Sunni militias ruled parts of the west, north, and east. Baghdad was a killing zone.

And we had no effective allies on the ground.

But America responded. Men and women volunteered to fight, then volunteered to fight again. We built up local allies, equipped them, and motivated them to stand their ground. We became, in the words of military historian Bing West, "the strongest tribe" in Iraq.[6]

On November 22, 2007, one of my coauthors, David French, flew into a small forward operating base in Diyala Province, Iraq, in a CH-47 helicopter. He and his unit flew because AQI (the forerunner to ISIS) controlled the roads leading into and out of their base. Had they driven, they would have been attacked by terrorists, and men likely would have died.

After almost a year of hard fighting and coalition building, his unit left that base, and this time they drove. AQI was gone, our Iraqi allies controlled the roads, and formerly devastated villages were springing back to life.

The jihadists were not invincible. They could be beaten. It just took courage and will.

Every time I fly into Israel, I'm moved by what I see. Israel is a beautiful land, where the desert has literally bloomed. As my plane comes in for a landing, I can see out my window row after row of beautiful houses where there used to be battlefields. In some places, farms stretch out as far as the eye can see, growing some of the most delicious fruit in the world.

I'm reminded that every single square inch of that land has been fought for against overwhelming odds. Every single square inch has been protected and reclaimed from those who tried—again and again—to finish what Hitler started.

The jihadists were not invincible. They could be beaten. It just took Israeli courage and will.

In New York, the Freedom Tower is finally nearing completion. This massive skyscraper, taller than the lost towers of the

World Trade Center, stands as a symbol of American strength. Knock us down, and we rebuild—taller, stronger, better. But while we can build buildings, sometimes the human heart can be more fragile. After thirteen years of war, do we still have the will? Our enemy certainly does. They are remorseless and savage, feeding on our weakness.

But they are not invincible. They can be beaten. It will just take American courage and American will.

CHAPTER TWELVE

NEW UPDATE: ISIS IS EXPANDING

In the summer of 2014, when we wrote the first edition of this book, we began with images—the power of pictures.

The images were of beheadings, the time-tested terror tactic of jihadists. These images had horrifying power. For the civilized world, they were too terrible to watch, and news organizations routinely cut away at the fateful moment—unwilling to subject their audiences to the horror of the kill.

But to jihadists and their tens of millions (perhaps even hundreds of millions[1]) of sympathizers, the images were energizing, even inspiring. To jihadists, beheadings of infidels are evidence of their fidelity to their faith and to their commitment to its cause. And they use these gruesome images as recruiting tools. To attract even more like-minded jihadists to their cause.

So, no one should have been surprised to see ISIS try to

ramp up the level of brutality and depravity. After all, it's what its public wants.

On Tuesday, February 3, 2015, ISIS released a video of Jordanian pilot Muath al-Kasaesbeh burned alive, in a cage.[2] Captured after his plane went down during a bombing raid over Syria, al-Kasaesbeh suffered a horrible, brutal death—with his murder set to music and staged for maximum propaganda impact. Once again, the jihadist world exulted—rejoicing in death and feeling empowered through terror and humiliation.

But this time, not everyone in the civilized world recoiled from the images. Despite howling protest, Fox News decided to show its audience precisely what ISIS does.[3] It ran the video of al-Kasaesbeh's execution, uncut.

For too long, the West has flinched in the face of jihadist brutality.

During the events of 9/11, television networks quickly decided to cut away from the images of Americans leaping to their deaths from the top floors of the World Trade Center—acts borne of ultimate desperation, in which men and women chose to jump rather than burn.

And the self-censorship has continued, with networks unwilling to show the world the true face of jihadist violence.

At the same time, politicians, including our president, have avoided actually describing the true nature of our enemy. Instead they've chosen to praise Islam while denying the Islamic faith of jihadists, believing that by concealing the truth they're currying favor with potential Muslim allies.[4]

In reality, however, we've gained no favor and have, instead, shown ourselves to be weak. Our leaders have done their best to lull the public into the belief that jihad represents the actions of a few extremists, and that there is no widespread support for jihad in the Muslim world. And in so doing, they render the public less likely to support the kinds of actions that are necessary to protect our nation, defeat jihad, and spare hundreds of thousands of innocents from violent death.

The first edition of this book was largely based on papers we presented at Oxford University's History, Politics and Society program on Religion and Politics in the Middle East in July 2014. Since that time, there have been dramatic new developments, in the Middle East and within ISIS, and those developments further emphasize the themes and warnings we published in the first edition.

One of the most important developments is that President Obama—finally realizing that ISIS is not the "JV Team"—has sent Congress a proposed Authorization for Use of Military Force (AUMF).[5]

Also, more research into ISIS has yielded new information about its explicitly religious motivations and use of ancient Islamic beliefs to motivate its contemporary followers.[6]

In addition, there is new cause to be concerned about our longstanding NATO ally Turkey, the only majority-Muslim nation in the Western alliance. Turkey, under increasing Islamist influence, is a gateway not only for Western recruits for ISIS but also for the black market oil that ISIS uses to sustain its considerable war chest.

And if that weren't dangerous enough, Turkey's Islamist

government is helping keep the virulently anti-Israel jihadist terrorist group Hamas alive through sustained public and private support.[7]

Against the backdrop of these recent events, we've updated this book to track new developments, outline emerging threats, and discuss what has worked—and what hasn't—as America and its allies respond to the most powerful jihadist army in centuries. We'll outline the changes that have taken place in the Middle East, Europe, and Africa. We'll look at the expansion of ISIS into new nations, and we'll examine ISIS's troubling success at recruiting volunteers from across the Western world.

Perhaps the most disturbing development has been the enduring power of ISIS's ideas and images to spread its influence in the majority-Muslim world and beyond, often inspiring homegrown jihadists to commit terror acts without any directive or communication from ISIS.

Consider the following:

In the United States—in Oklahoma—a Muslim man beheaded fifty-four-year-old Colleen Hufford where she worked, and he started to behead a second woman before he was shot. Before launching his personal jihad, he posted a beheading video on his Facebook page and commented:

"This [sic] do we find the clear precedent that explains the particular penchant of Islamic terrorists to behead their victims, it is merely another precedent bestowed by their Prophet." He also added a citation from the Quran: "I will instill terror into the hearts of the Unbelievers; smite ye about their necks."[8]

In Canada, a Muslim man killed a soldier at a war memorial, then actually breached the Canadian parliament building before he was shot and killed. This attack occurred just two days after a different Muslim man hit two Canadian soldiers with his car, killing one.

Both attackers had expressed support for ISIS and jihad, and the Canadian prime minister called the parliament attack "ISIL-inspired" (using the alternative acronym for ISIS).[9]

In Sydney, Australia, a "self-styled Muslim cleric" assaulted a café, took hostages, and killed two before he himself was gunned down when Australian authorities stormed the building. A known radical, he unfurled an ISIS-style black flag of jihad during the initial siege.[10]

In France, a series of attacks shook Europe as jihadist gunmen stormed the offices of Charlie Hebdo, a satirical publication known for publishing images offensive to Muslims (and, for that matter, people of many other faiths), including cartoons of the Prophet Mohammed. They killed twelve people and left eleven others wounded. This attack launched a series of clashes as a different gunman seized a kosher market, where he killed four people and held fifteen others hostage before French police ended the siege.

(Incredibly, President Obama declared that the Islamic terrorist "randomly" shot people at the kosher market when the attack was clearly aimed at Jews. As one reporter noted, "If a guy goes into a kosher market and starts shooting it up, he's not looking for Buddhists, is he?")[11]

Even though the jihadist attackers proclaimed their allegiance to al-Qaeda in Yemen, there were indications that ISIS jihadists knew the attack was imminent and even tweeted chilling messages the day before the attack.[12]

In Denmark, a Muslim gunman launched a hail of bullets into a coffee shop that was hosting a free speech forum, killing two. Just before he launched his attack, he "swore fidelity to ISIS leader Abu Bakr Al-Baghdadi" in a Facebook post.[13]

As shocking as these attacks were, far more ominous developments were unfolding in Africa and the Middle East. In February 2015, ISIS released one of its most gruesome videos yet, showing the beheading of twenty-one Egyptian Coptic Christians on a beach in Libya.[14]

The video was grisly—once again showing ISIS's commitment to gruesome mass murder—but it was ominous as well: ISIS was now spreading without even conquering new territory. Its Islamic ideas and its savage atrocities were enough to win jihadist groups to their side. And now, ISIS has affiliates in Libya.

But that's not all. Egypt's "most active jihadist group," Ansar Beit al-Maqdis, has pledged allegiance to ISIS and is locked in a fierce struggle with the Egyptian army in the Sinai.[15] This places a branch of ISIS directly adjacent to Israel and its terrorists within striking distance of Israeli communities.

But the most dangerous expansion came in March 2015, when the Nigerian jihadist group Boko Haram joined with ISIS.[16] Located far from ISIS's Syrian and Iraqi strongholds, Boko Haram is one of the world's most powerful jihadist armies, controlling thousands of square miles of Nigerian territory, where it has launched a reign of terror matched only by ISIS's own.

Boko Haram burns villages, massacres their inhabitants, burns churches, kidnaps girls for slavery on a massive scale, and indulges in every form of war crime imaginable. The Nigerian government has been largely helpless to stop Boko Haram's expansion, and now Boko Haram carries the enormous psychological power of ISIS affiliation, placing Nigeria firmly within the worldwide jihadist movement.

As pre-existing jihadist groups pledge their loyalty to ISIS, individual Muslims are flocking to ISIS by the tens of thousands. The *Washington Post* published a graphic showing the inflow of foreign fighters to ISIS, and the numbers are sobering, with 130 from the U.S. and 100 from Canada alone.[17] The numbers from Western Europe are even higher—600 from Great Britain, 600 from Germany, 1,200 from France, 440 from Belgium, with hundreds more from other countries in our European alliance.[18]

As of the time of this update, roughly a thousand foreign fighters arrive in Syria each month, heeding the call of ISIS's ninety thousand social media messages per day.[19]

Yet, while ISIS is expanding, it is not invulnerable. With the right strategy, it will fall, and recent events show how.

CHAPTER THIRTEEN

ISIS IS VULNERABLE

ISIS's expansions and attacks demonstrate not only its incredible power—its conquests and brutality—but also its ideas. Since the initial publication of this book, the Obama administration's unwillingness to acknowledge ISIS's thoroughly Islamic character has only grown more ridiculous—and more dangerous.

We can't truly defeat ISIS until we understand its beliefs, but once we understand, the path to victory grows clear.

In March, *The Atlantic* published a blockbuster cover story that utterly demolished any attempt to write Islam out of ISIS.[1] By Graeme Wood, a lecturer at Yale University, it not only described ISIS's theological doctrine but also noted how it tracks with historical Islamic teaching—teaching that traces its origins back to Islam's founding. It was astonishing to read—in a mainstream liberal publication—statements like this:

> But Muslims who call the Islamic State un-Islamic are typically, as the Princeton scholar Bernard Haykel, the

leading expert on the group's theology, told me, "embarrassed and politically correct, with a cotton-candy view of their own religion" that neglects "what their religion has historically and legally required." Many denials of the Islamic State's religious nature, he said, are rooted in an "interfaith-Christian-nonsense tradition."[2]

And this:

According to Haykel, the ranks of the Islamic State are deeply infused with religious vigor. Koranic quotations are ubiquitous. "Even the foot soldiers spout this stuff constantly," Haykel said. "They mug for their cameras and repeat their basic doctrines in formulaic fashion, and they do it all the time." He regards the claim that the Islamic State has distorted the texts of Islam as preposterous, sustainable only through willful ignorance. "People want to absolve Islam," he said. "It's this 'Islam is a religion of peace' mantra. As if there is such a thing as 'Islam'! It's what Muslims do, and how they interpret their texts." Those texts are shared by all Sunni Muslims, not just the Islamic State. "And these guys have just as much legitimacy as anyone else."[3]

While our book focused primarily on ISIS's announced geopolitical and military goals, Wood examines how these geopolitical goals flow directly from its version of Islam. Goals that—critically—include the necessity of capturing and holding ground. While a competing jihadist group like al-Qaeda can and does operate in the shadows, a Caliphate requires territory, and if the Caliphate stops expanding—or suffers battlefield losses that even shrink its reach—it can lose its authority and legitimacy.[4] As we explained earlier in this book, a Caliphate is a physical place—historically an empire in which spiritual and political authority are combined under one supreme ruler, the caliph. Just as nations require territory, so does a Caliphate.

As Wood says, "Caliphates cannot exist as underground movements." If ISIS loses its territory, "all those oaths of allegiance are no longer binding."[5] Thus, it becomes entirely possible that if ISIS loses its territory in Iraq and Syria, the movement itself will fracture with other jihadist groups drifting away, leaving tens of thousands of potential Muslim jihadists in the West and elsewhere no longer compelled to join ISIS on the ground or inspired to fight in their own backyard.

And we now have evidence that even as ISIS still maintains its religious potency, internal strains may be emerging within the movement on its home ground—in those limited spaces where American military might, combined with attacks from local allies like the Kurds, have checked their advance.

On March 8, 2015, the *Washington Post* reported—citing "activists and residents of areas under Islamic State [ISIS] control"—that while ISIS had only suffered military setbacks at the "fringes of its territory," even those limited reverses are having disproportionate internal effect.[6] Echoing Graeme Wood's piece, the *Post* noted that ISIS struggles when its "grandiose promises collide with realities on the ground." The

Post quoted Lina Khatib, the director of the Carnegie Middle East Center in Beirut:

> "The key challenge facing ISIS right now is more internal than external," she said, using another term for the group. "We're seeing basically a failure of the central tenet of ISIS ideology, which is to unify people of different origins under the caliphate. This is not working on the ground. It is making them less effective in governing and less effective in military operations."[7]

In other words, even modest reverses can have disproportionate impact. After all, if strains are becoming apparent after months of limited aerial bombardment combined with small-scale counteroffensives with Kurdish troops (and others) that have cost ISIS only 20 percent of its Iraqi territory,[8] how much more effective and devastating would a truly large-scale effort be?

We actually know the answer. As we noted in the first edition of this book, Americans have confronted—and largely defeated—ISIS before, during the Surge in Iraq in 2007–2008. At the start of the Surge, al-Qaeda in Iraq, the precursor to ISIS, controlled large sections of Iraq. Indeed, it had even declared Diyala Province to be the "Islamic State of Iraq."

A massive, concerted American and Iraqi effort yanked control of this territory from al-Qaeda, killed thousands of militants, and left its remnants largely powerless. These combined forces did it through a strategy of "clear, hold, and build," which entailed taking territory, holding it against counter-attacks, and building a sustainable security infrastructure.

"Clear, hold, and build" works; it worked in the Surge and it worked at key points in the Vietnam War. Yet it's a strategy that fails when there is a lack of commitment—when forces "clear and hold" temporarily but don't sustain the commitment to "build." Just as politics caused America to abandon its South Vietnamese allies in 1975, so did politics lead President Obama to prematurely pull American troops out of Iraq in 2011—before they could build.

Just at the moment when commitment is most necessary—when we are seeing the first fruits of American military engagement—the president of the United States has proven that he's not in the fight for the long haul.

How do we know this? He's trying to write his lack of commitment into law.

In early 2015, President Obama submitted to Congress a draft Authorization for the Use of Military Force (AUMF) against ISIS.[9] While the notion of essentially declaring war on ISIS is constitutionally and strategically sound—signaling a national commitment to defeating our dangerous enemy—the document itself is fatally flawed, and the flaws are apparent from the first sentence.

The resolution begins with a declaration of purpose: "To authorize the limited use of the United States Armed Forces against the Islamic State of Iraq and the Levant."[10] The core intention is evident from the beginning—American efforts are to be limited, against an enemy that is itself capable of limitless savagery. The AUMF then goes on to propose specific limitations that:

Exclude the use of American troops in "enduring offensive ground combat operations";

Limit the authority to fight to three years;

Repeal the much broader AUMF that launched the Iraq War and still grants American forces the legal right to fight in Iraq today.

In other words, the AUMF President Obama proposes is less an "authorization" for the use of force than it is a "limit" on the use of force.

In the first edition of this book, we proposed a formula for military success—equip proven Muslim allies and assist them with enough American force to ensure victory. Because the ultimate solution for defeating ISIS has to come from Muslims (after all, America cannot, and should not, occupy every inch of ground contested by jihadists), we have to ensure that our Muslim allies are stronger than their jihadist enemies. Because we can't risk defeat for those allies—or any further victories by ISIS—we have to be ready to apply enough American power in every conflict to make a decisive difference.

And we do not lack for Muslim allies. Since the first edition of our book, we've seen the Kurds in Iraq and Syria fight bravely and effectively to stop ISIS advances and win the key battle of Kobane. We've seen the Jordanian Air Force launch effective attacks in retaliation for the burning death of their pilot. And—critically—the most powerful Arab nation in the world, Egypt, is proposing the creation of an "Arab ready force" to defeat ISIS and other jihadists.[11]

Indeed, Egypt not only has taken strong action against the Muslim Brotherhood and other jihadists within its borders but has also turned strongly against Hamas, demonstrating greater solidarity with Israel in its most recent war in Gaza than the Obama administration did.

We have powerful and motivated Muslim allies. We have a military that ISIS can't hope to match. With these assets, the president should take the following steps:

Submit a "clean" AUMF to Congress—one that authorizes the use of force against ISIS without limiting either this president or the next. Let the commander-in-chief, in cooperation with his generals, decide how to defeat the enemy. Don't limit his freedom of action.

Retain the present AUMF that authorizes the use of force in Iraq. So long as U.S. national security interests are implicated by conflict in Iraq, we need to maintain our freedom of action.

Provide willing and proven allies (such as the Kurds, Jordanians, Egyptians, and select units of the Iraqi Armed Forces) with the weapons, training, and direct support they need. Support to defeat not just ISIS but also any rival effort from Iranian-backed militias to seize and hold ground. After all, it is hardly a true "victory" if ISIS loses and Iran wins.

Withhold all military support from any Iranian-allied militia or any Iranian forces on the ground in Iraq.

Remove limits on American forces currently on the ground in Iraq so that they may effectively assist our Iraqi allies.

Recent history has proven that allied forces operate better when American forces are present and able to provide direct support. So far, among the Western powers, apparently only Canadian troops have engaged in direct ground combat with ISIS.[12]

Reinforce American forces as needed to protect the force and to guarantee allied military success.

The president's plan, by contrast, prioritizes limits over victory— rendering defeat not just possible, but probable.

Make no mistake; our enemies are counting on our foolishness and inconstancy. After Graeme Wood wrote his blockbuster article, he reported that ISIS's social media indicated he'd gotten the story exactly right, that he'd pegged ISIS's apocalyptic Muslim worldview.[13] He also discovered something else: at least some ISIS supporters are actually happy that President Obama won't call them Muslim. An ISIS supporter wrote Wood to explain:

> What stands out to me that others don't seem to discuss much, is how the Islamic State, Osama [bin Laden] and others are operating as if they are reading from a script that was written 1,400 years ago. They not only follow these prophecies, but plan ahead based upon them. One would therefore assume that the enemies of Islam would note this and prepare adequately, but [it's] almost as if they feel that playing along would mean that they believe in the prophecies too, and so they ignore them

and go about things their own way. . . . [The] enemies of the Muslims may be aware of what the Muslims are planning, but it won't benefit them at all as they prefer to either keep their heads in the sand, or to fight their imaginary war based upon rational freedom-loving democrats vs. irrational evil terrorist madmen. With this in mind, maybe you can understand to some degree one of the reasons why many Muslims will share your piece. It's not because we don't understand what it is saying in terms of how to defeat the Muslims, rather it's because we know that those in charge will ignore it and screw things up anyway.[14]

In other words, the enemy has told us his plans and intentions, and we should plan accordingly. The enemy, however, knows of our slavish devotion to political correctness and has confidence that we won't act on our knowledge, that we won't have the necessary staying power, and that we will—once again—snatch defeat from the jaws of victory.

CHAPTER FOURTEEN

TURKEY: THE POWERFUL WILD CARD[1]

In 2014, the ACLJ launched its Oxford Centre for the Study of Law & Public Policy. The Centre's purpose is to analyze geopolitical trends from legal, human rights, and policy perspectives. The Centre's 2014 sessions yielded a comprehensive series of papers that formed the foundation of this book. Our focus on ISIS and its jihadist cousin, Hamas, proved to be sadly necessary—as Israel yet again fought its own war against Hamas while ISIS achieved victory after victory in Syria and Iraq.

In 2015, the Centre is focusing on the emerging challenge of Turkey—a NATO ally possessing the most powerful and well-trained army in the Muslim world, one of the largest economies in the region, and a long shared border with Syria and Iraq.

Simply put, if Turkey strongly supports the effort against ISIS, the alliance becomes overwhelmingly powerful. If Turkey sits on the sidelines or—even worse—tacitly sides with jihadists, the fight becomes immeasurably more difficult.

While Turkey is not often in the news, it's critical that we examine its actions thus far. Led by an Islamist president, Recep Tayyip Erdoğan, and increasingly allied with such jihadist organizations as Hamas, its response to ISIS has been underwhelming at best and alarming at worst.

In September 2014, five U.N. Security Council permanent members, a number of European and Arab countries, and representatives from the European Union, Arab League, and United Nations met at an international counterterrorism conference in Paris.[2] Every nation except Turkey pledged to support the Baghdad government in its fight against ISIS.[3] Turkey claimed that its reluctance to openly support efforts against ISIS was due to ISIS's kidnapping of forty-six Turkish citizens and three Iraqis from Turkey's Consulate General in Mosul in June 2014.[4]

Also, in September 2014, while ten NATO countries (Britain, Australia, Canada, Denmark, France, Germany, Italy, Poland, the United States, and Turkey) formed a coalition to destroy ISIS,[5] President Erdoğan did not elaborate how Turkey would contribute to the coalition's fight against ISIS.[6] Then, in late September, ISIS released the Turkish hostages, showing uncharacteristic mercy.[7]

In October 2014, after the hostages were released, the Turkish government did authorize the use of military force against ISIS.[8] At the same time, however, President Erdoğan initially refused to allow Kurdish fighters to enter Syria through Turkey to fight ISIS.[9] Instead, Turkey attacked installations of the Kurdistan Workers Party (PKK) in the southeast, near the Iraqi border.[10] It was not until late October that Turkey allowed "a limited number of Iraqi Kurdish members of the peshmerga to cross from Turkey into Kobani, Syria, to fight" ISIS.[11]

After attacking the PKK and providing limited aid to the Peshmerga, Turkey continued to send mixed messages. On the one hand, it agreed to train moderate Syrian rebels (those in the Syrian civil war against the Assad regime) on its soil.[12] At the same time, however, it was reported that Turkey had allowed ISIS fighters to travel through Turkish territory to join the fight against the Kurds.[13] A former ISIS fighter explained in an interview after he escaped from ISIS that ISIS commanders claim they had full cooperation from the Turks.[14] Reports from the National Army of Syrian Kurdistan further allege that the "Turkish army gives IS terrorists weapons, ammunition and allows them to cross the Turkish official border crossings."[15] There is yet no independent evidence, however, to support these claims.[16]

Inaction against ISIS has fueled suspicion, especially among Turkey's Kurdish population, that the Turkish government "made a secret agreement with ISIS to 'clean up' Kobani [the Kurdish Syrian stronghold recently defended from ISIS attack]."[17] There are good reasons for these suspicions. First, while ISIS has beheaded or burned to death American, British, Japanese, and Jordanian hostages, it released all Turkish hostages in September 2014.[18] This action raises suspicion that a deal was made in exchange for the hostages.[19] President Erdoğan denied that ISIS released hostages in exchange for a promise to support ISIS and said that it was a "covert rescue operation."[20] Yet Turkish Prime Minister Ahmet Davutoğlu said that the hostages were released as a "result of the intelligence agency's 'own methods' and not a special forces operation."[21] These inconsistent statements have raised concerns about Turkey's relationship with ISIS.[22]

Second, within its borders, Turkey seems to have allowed the recruitment of ISIS militants, medical treatment for militants, and the free movement of militants from Syria to Turkey and back again.[23] U.S. law enforcement caught Americans en route to Turkey, believing they could join ISIS via Turkey.[24] Additionally, United States counterterrorism officials warned Turkey that ISIS militants have terrorist sleeper cells in Istanbul, Ankara, and Konya.[25] ISIS "sleeper cells" are created when, instead of joining the visible fight in Iraq and Syria, ISIS supporters remain inconspicuously in their country of origin, leaving them with the ability to attack at an unexpected time.[26] U.S. officials believe there are also sleeper cells in Van, Diyarbakir, Hatay, and Gazinatep.[27] Despite the Turkish government's knowledge of ISIS sleeper cells in the country, Turkey remains elusive on the role it will play in the NATO coalition's fight.[28]

Third, even after the Turkish hostages were released, Turkey has not only been reluctant to fight ISIS in Syria, but it has—incredibly enough—even been reluctant to condemn ISIS's actions.[29]

Additionally, as long as ISIS is not an immediate security threat to Turkey, Turkey can benefit financially from the "black economy" that funds ISIS.[30] A huge part of ISIS's financial strength comes from oil smuggling to neighboring countries.[31] ISIS can smuggle over thirty thousand barrels of crude oil a day at a price of twenty-five to sixty dollars per barrel.[32] It sells its oil to intermediaries in Syria, who then transport the oil to refineries in Turkey and Iran.[33] The U.S. government has been unable to convince "Turkey to stop the black market trade of oil from ISIS into Turkey."[34]

Finally—and crucially—although Turkey is a NATO member with the desire to become an EU member, Islamist leadership governs it. ISIS, Hamas, and other terrorist organizations interpret Islamic teachings in ways similar to President Erdoğan himself. Indeed, President Erdoğan has proven to be among Hamas's most valuable allies.

ISIS shares a version of President Erdoğan's faith, it shares President Erdoğan's enemies, and it enriches Turkey. Is it any wonder that rational people doubt our NATO ally's loyalty?

THE COST OF STALEMATE

When we wrote the first edition of this book, we received some criticism for including sections about Hamas. Yet Hamas presents precisely the right case study in context. Not only does it share ISIS's extreme brutality (for example, Hamas killed its enemies by throwing them from buildings long before ISIS began the practice[1]), it presents a model for the world that shows what happens when jihadists take and hold territory—a model of death, despair, and eternal conflict.

It is for this reason that the prime minister of Israel, Benjamin Netanyahu, declared to the U.N. General Assembly that "ISIS and Hamas are branches of the same poisonous tree," and properly noted "[w]hen it comes to their ultimate goals,

Hamas is ISIS and ISIS is Hamas. And what they share in common, all militant Islamists share in common."[2]

Even after losing its summer 2014 fight with Israel, Hamas continues to rule Gaza with an iron fist, and the human costs are immense. Innocent civilians live among piles of rubble, working to scrape out a living in the ruins of a once-vibrant city. Meanwhile, Hamas will not yield, and the politically correct international community will not allow Israel to root it out once and for all—leaving nothing but perpetual war, perpetual suffering, and perpetual misery.

And until jihad is defeated, jihadists will proliferate—hopeful that they will win the long struggle. On March 7, 2015, the *New York Times*' Nicholas Kristof published a poignant piece outlining the costs of stalemate, of endless war. In it, he described not just the plight of the innocents but also the hate of the jihadists, including young men growing up to take their turn trying to kill Israelis. He talked to Ahmed, a teenager training to fight:

> Ahmed keeps a poster of a family friend who was killed while firing rockets at Israel, and he says he yearns to do the same. I asked him how he could possibly favor more warfare after all the bloodshed Gaza had endured, and he shrugged.
>
> "Maybe we can kill all of them, and then it will get better," he said. I asked him if he really wanted to wipe out all of Israel, and he nodded. "I will give my soul to kill all Israelis," he said.[3]

Yet in spite of this relentless hate, as of the publication of this update, there is some reason for limited optimism in the fight against ISIS. It has been largely stopped on the ground in Iraq. It is no longer rampaging at will through Syria. And there are plans for serious counteroffensives—at least in Iraq—to retake the city of Mosul.

However, there are no serious plans to retake ISIS-held lands in Syria. ISIS-allied Boko Haram continues to rampage through Nigeria. Jihadists (including ISIS allies) control large sections of Libya.

But President Obama seeks to limit American force, continues to deprive allies of the resources they need, and tries to place deadlines on warfare. Yet our enemies place no deadlines on their efforts. They fight until they can fight no more.

Before Vietnam, American political leaders—from Lincoln to Wilson to Roosevelt—understood that fighting to win was ultimately humane, that victories meant an end to a conflict. It is time that we restore that great American military tradition—a tradition of strength and victory, not of stalemate and doubt.

The alternative is the intolerable reality of the present, where war grinds on with no end in sight, where Christianity faces extinction in the very region of its birth, where Israel faces never-ending generations of genocidal terrorists, and where a great power—the United States—again and again shows itself to be a faithless friend with a weak will.

We ended the first edition with a word of hope, with the

declaration that we can defeat jihad, that victory simply requires "American courage and American will."

We end this new edition with a word of warning. When American will is lacking, and American courage is not deployed, a bloody stalemate is the best-case scenario. The worst-case is unthinkable—a new genocide in the Middle East, bombs at home, and a brand of radical Islam ascendant—inspiring warfare for generations to come.

Given that option, courage and will are our only hope. We must not turn our back on these great American virtues. We cannot hide from our responsibilities, and we cannot be intimidated by even the most horrifying of images. It's time for America's leaders to stop flinching in the face of terror. It's time for America's leaders to step up, to inspire a great people to victory.

It's once again time for America to lead.

ACKNOWLEDGMENTS

It goes without saying that the effort to take the papers that we submitted at Oxford University and convert them into a book in a six-week period was a Herculean task. This would not have been possible without input from colleagues Professor Harry Hutchison and Dr. Andrew Ekonomou, both of whom serve as Visiting Fellows at Harris Manchester College, University of Oxford, and both co-founders of the Oxford Centre for the Study of Law and Public Policy. This book represents the Centre's first official publication.

We gained valuable insight in our participation during our time at Exeter College, Oxford, with Prof. Dr. Farhang Jahanpour, specifically on the issue of ISIS.

And last, but certainly not least, our editor at Simon & Schuster/Howard Books, Becky Nesbitt, who worked quickly and tirelessly in editing this work.

To download "Where I Stand," an exclusive track
from the Jay Sekulow Band, visit whereistandsong.com
and enter the password "hope."

NOTES

FOREWORD

1. Martin Matishak, "Republican: ISIS Developing the Means to 'Blow Up' an American City," *Hill*, August 21, 2014, http://thehill.com/policy/defense/215684-republican-isis -developing-means-to-blow-up-an-american-city.

CHAPTER ONE. THE HORROR OF JIHAD

1. Steve Bird, "So Wicked That Even Al Qaeda Disowned Them: Letter Found at Bin Laden's Hideout Warned of Islamic State's Extreme Brutality," *Daily Mail*, August 10, 2014, http://www.dailymail.co.uk/news/article-2721417 /So-wicked-Al-Qaeda-disowned-Letter-Bin-Ladens-hideout -warned-Islamic-States-extreme-brutality.html.

2. Terrence McCoy, "ISIS Just Stole $425 million, Iraqi Governor Says, and Became the 'World's Richest Terrorist Group,'" *Washington Post*, June 10, 2014, http://www .washingtonpost.com/news/morning-mix/wp/2014/06/12 /isis-just-stole-425-million-and-became-the-worlds-richest -terrorist-group/.

3. Terrence McCoy, "Islamic State 'Now Controls Resources and Territory Unmatched in the History of Extremist

Organizations,'" *Washington Post*, August 4, 2014, http://www
.washingtonpost.com/news/morning-mix/wp/2014/08/04
/islamic-state-now-controls-resources-and-territory
-unmatched-in-history-of-extremist-organizations/.

4. Tom Coghlan and Deborah Haynes, "Fear of Dirty Bomb as
ISIS Rebels Seize Radioactive Uranium in Iraq," *Australian*,
July 11, 2014.

5. Michael Daly, "ISIS Leader: 'See You in New York,'"
Daily Beast, June 14, 2014, http://www.thedailybeast
.com/articles/2014/06/14/isis-leader-see-you-in-new-york.html.

6. "New ISIS Video: 'We Will Raise Black Flag Over
White House,'" Fox News Insider, August 8, 2014,
http://foxnewsinsider.com/2014/08/08/new-isis-video
-%E2%80%98we-will-raise-black-flag-over-white-house%
E2%80%99.

7. See Sanjay Sanghoee, "What ISIS and Hamas Have in
Common," *Huffington Post*, August 7, 2014, http://www
.huffingtonpost.com/sanjay-sanghoee/what-hamas-and-isis
-have_b_5660020.html.

CHAPTER TWO. THE RISE OF ISIS AND THE NEW CALIPHATE

1. Majid Khadduri, *War and Peace in the Law of Islam* (Clark, NJ:
Lawbook Exchange, 2010), 48.

2. Ibid., 4, 17.

3. Ibid., 158.

4. Ibid., 16.

5. Ibid., 26.

6. Ibid., 156.

7. Ibid., 155.

8. Ibid., 170–71.

9. Ibid., 64.

10. Ibid.

11. Ibid., 16–17.

12. Majid Khadduri and Herbert J. Liebesny, eds., *Law in the
Middle East* (Clark, NJ: Lawbook Exchange, 2009), 3.

13. Ibid., 14.

14. Ibid., 3.
15. Khadduri, *War and Peace in the Law of Islam*, 11.
16. Khadduri and Liebesny, eds., *Law in the Middle East*, 5.
17. Ibid., 14.
18. Khadduri, *War and Peace in the Law of Islam*, 10.
19. Khadduri and Liebesny, eds., *Law in the Middle East*, 4.
20. Ibid., 6.
21. Ibid., 6, 8.
22. Juan E. Campo, ed., Encyclopedia of Islam (New York: Facts on File, 2009), 33.
23. Ibid.
24. Ibid.
25. Khadduri and Liebesny, eds., *Law in the Middle East*, 114.
26. Ibid.
27. Paul Sullivan, "Why Should We Care About the Iraqi Shia?," History News Network, April 13, 2004, http://hnn.us /article/1455.
28. Karl Vick, "What Is the Caliphate," *Time*, July 1, 2014, http:// time.com/2942239/what-is-the-caliphate/.
29. Ibid.
30. Juan Jose Valdes et al., "Iraq: 1,200 Years of Turbulent History in Five Maps," *National Geographic*, July 2, 2014, http://news .nationalgeographic.com/news/2014/07/140702-iraq-history -maps/.
31. Vick, "What Is the Caliphate."
32. Omar Khalidi, "The Caliph's Daughter," *Cornucopia*, http:// www.cornucopia.net/magazine/articles/the-caliphs-daughter/.
33. Ibid.
34. Ibid.
35. Vick, "What Is the Caliphate."
36. Bylaws of the International Muslim Brotherhood, ch. II, art. II § E, http://www.investigativeproject.org/documents /misc/673.pdf.
37. Tim Lister, "How ISIS Is Overshadowing Al Qaeda," CNN, June 30, 2014, http://www.cnn. com/2014/06/30/world/meast /isis-overshadows-al-qaeda/.

38. ISIS stands for Islamic State of Iraq and Syria. It can also mean Islamic State of Iraq and Greater Syria or Islamic State of Iraq and *Sham*. Although ISIS has recently adopted the name "Islamic State," we will call it ISIS in this paper because that is the better-known name.

39. ISIL stands for Islamic State of Iraq and the Levant.

40. See Amir Abdallah, "Urgent Video: Isis Releases Abu Bakr Al-Baghdadi Sermon In Mosul Grand Mosque," Iraqi News, July 5, 2014, http://www.iraqinews.com/features/urgent-video-isis-releases-abu-bakr-al-baghdadi-sermon-mosul-grand-mosque/ (emphasis added). Note that the full-length video of the sermon had English subtitles. The language quoted above is directly transcribed from the video's English subtitles. Grammatical and typographical errors have not been corrected. Quran cite is 25:55.

41. "Wanted Abu Du'a Up to $10 Million," Rewards for Justice, http://www.webcitation.org/62Hxw9AqD. He is known to have used a number of aliases, such as Dr. Ibrahim 'Awwad Ibrahim 'Ali al-Badri al-Samarrai', Ibrahim 'Awad Ibrahim al-Badri al Samarrai, Abu Duaa', Dr. Ibrahim, and Abu Bakr al-Baghdadi. Ibid.

42. Graeme Baker, "The Fierce Ambition of ISIL's Baghdadi," Al Jazeera, June 15, 2014, http://www. aljazeera.com/news/middleeast/2014/06/fierce-ambition-isil-baghdadi-2014612142242188464.html.

43. Ibid.

44. Ibid.

45. Ibid.

46. "Profile: Islamic State in Iraq and the Levant (ISIS)," BBC News, June 16, 2014, http://www.bbc.com/news/world-middle-east-24179084.

47. See http://icasualties.org/Iraq/index.aspx.

48. "Profile: Islamic State in Iraq and the Levant (ISIS)," BBC News, June 16, 2014, http://www.bbc.com/news/world-middle-east-24179084.

49. Ibid.
50. Ibid.
51. Ibid.
52. Ibid.
53. McCoy, "ISIS Just Stole $425 Million, Iraqi Governor Says."
54. "Jordan's Abu Qatada: Caliphate Declaration 'Void,'" *Daily Star*, July 15, 2014, http://www.dailystar. com.lb/News /Middle-East/2014/Jul-15/263931-jordans-abu-qatada -caliphate-declaration-void.ashx#axzz37qB7TbEF.
55. Alhayat Media Center, "This Is the Promise of Allah," https://ia902505.us.archive.org/28/items/poa_25984/EN.pdf, 5 (emphasis added). Al-Jazeera has reported the foregoing document to be an official ISIS publication. "Sunni Rebels Declare New 'Islamic Caliphate,'" Al Jazeera, June 30, 2014, http://www.aljazeera.com/news/middleeast/2014/06/isil -declares-new-islamic-caliphate-201462917326669749.html.

CHAPTER THREE. ISIS: THE WORLD'S MOST RUTHLESS AND POWERFUL JIHADIST ARMY

1. Liz Sly, "Al-Qaeda Disavows Any Ties with Radical Islamist Isis Group in Syria, Iraq," *Washington Post*, February 3, 2013, http://www.washingtonpost.com/world/middle_east/al-qaeda -disavows-any-ties-with-radical-islamist-isis-group-in-syria -iraq/2014/02/03/2c9afc3a-8cef-11e3-98ab-fe5228217bd1 _story.html; Elisa Oddon, "Jordanian Jihadist Leader Condemns Isis Caliphate," Al Monitor, July 7, 2014, http:// www.al-monitor.com/pulse/ru/originals/ 2014/07/jordan -maqdisi-jihad-iraq-isis-caliphate-qaeda.html; Ellen Knickmeyer, "Al Qaeda 'Disavows' Syrian Terror Group for Being Too Terroristy," *Wall Street Journal*, February 3, 2014, http://online.wsj.com/news/articles/ SB1000142 405270230485110457936104192884318. See also Basma Atassi, "Qaeda Chief Annuls Syrian-Iraqi Jihad Merger," Al Jazeera, June 9, 2013, http://www.aljazeera.com/news/ middleeast/2013/06/ 2013699425657882.html.

2. Abdullah Yusuf Ali, *The Meaning of the Holy Qur'an*, 10th ed. (1999; reprint, n.p.: Amana, 2004), 4:93.

3. Ibid., 6:151.

4. Ahmad ibn Naqib al-Misri, *Reliance of the Traveller*, rev. ed., trans. Nuh Ha Mim Keller (N.p.: Amana, 2008), 583 (1368).

5. Ibid.

6. Vol. 1, Bk. 2, No. 9, Sahih Bukhari, http://www.sahih -bukhari.com/Pages/Bukhari_1_02.php.

7. Vol. 1, Bk. 2, No. 10, Sahih Bukhari, http://www.sahih -bukhari.com/Pages/Bukhari_1_02.php.

8. Vol. 1, Bk. 2, No. 46, Sahih Bukhari, http://www.sahih -bukhari.com/Pages/Bukhari_1_02.php.

9. Amnesty International, "Rule of Fear: ISIS Abuses in Detention in Northern Syria," December 19, 2013, 6–7, http://www.amnesty.org/en/library/asset/MDE24/063/2013 /en/32d380a3-cc47-4cb6-869f2628ca44cb99/mde 240632013en.pdf.

10. Ibid.

11. Ibid., 7.

12. "Abuse 'Rife in Secret Al-Qaeda Jails in Syria,'" BBC News, December 19, 2013, http://www.bbc.com/news/world-middle -east-25440381.

13. Amnesty International, "Rule of Fear," 1.

14. Ibid., 7.

15. Ibid.

16. Ibid.

17. Ibid.

18. Ibid., 9.

19. Ibid., 10.

20. Salma Abdelaziz, "Death and Desecration in Syria: Jihadist Group 'Crucifies' Bodies to Send Message," CNN, May 2, 2014, http://www.cnn.com/2014/05/01/world/meast/syria -bodies-crucifixions/.

21. Ibid.

22. Ibid.

23. Ibid.
24. "Syria: ISIS Summarily Killed Civilians," Human Rights Watch, June 14, 2014, http://www.hrw.org/news/ 2014/06/14 /syria-isis-summarily-killed-civilians.
25. Ibid.
26. Adam Lusher, "Iraq Crisis: The Footage That Shows Isis Militants Taunting and Killing Shia Soldiers," *Independent*, June 16, 2014, http://www.independent.co.uk/news/world /middle-east/iraq-crisis-the-footage-that-shows-isis-militants -taunting-and-killing-shia-forces-9541929.html.
27. Ibid.
28. Rod Nordland and Alyssa J. Rubin, "Massacre Claim Shakes Iraq," *New York Times*, June 15, 2014, http://www.nytimes .com/2014/06/16/world/middleeast/iraq.html?_r=3; see also "Militants Post Grisly Images of Mass Killing in Iraq," CBS News, June 15, 2014, http://www.cbsnews.com/news/iraq -conflict-isis-militants-post-grisly-images-of-mass-killing/.
29. Connor Simpson, "Rights Group Confirms ISIS Mass Grave Images," *Wire*, June 27, 2014, http://www.thewire .com/global/2014/06/rights-group-confirms-isis-mass-grave -images/373598/.
30. Simon Tomlinson and Amy White, "'This Is Our Football, It's Made of Skin #World Cup': After Posting Sickening Beheading Video of Iraqi Policeman, Isis Boast of Slaughtering 1,700 Soldiers," *Daily Mail*, June 13, 2014, http:// www.dailymail.co.uk/news/article-2656905/ISIS-jihadists -seize-two-towns-bear-Baghdad-U-S-tanks-helicopters -stolen-fleeing-western-trained-Iraqi-forces.html. See also Chris Hughes et al., "Police Chief Beheaded By Jihadist Rebels Who Tweeted: 'This Is Our Ball. It Is Made of Skin. #World Cup,'" *Mirror*, June 14, 2014, http://www.mirror.co .uk/news/world-news/police-chief-beheaded-jihadist-rebels -3690513.
31. Ibid.
32. Ibid.

33. Convention (IV) Relative to the Protection of Civilian Persons in Time of War, art. 16, August 12, 1949, 6 U.S.T. 3316, 75 U.N.T.S. 135.

34. Sam Greenhill et al., "Isis Butchers Leave 'Roads Lined with Decapitated Police and Soldiers': Battle for Baghdad Looms as Thousands Answer Iraqi Government's Call to Arms and Jihadists Bear Down on Capital," *Daily Mail*, June 12, 2014, http://www.dailymail.co.uk/news/article-2655977/ISIS -militants-march-Baghdad-trademark-bullet-head-gets-way -control-north.html.

35. Tomlinson and White, "'This Is Our Football.'"

36. Vasudevan Sridharan, "Iraq Isis Crisis: Judge Who Sentenced Saddam Hussein to Death Executed by Rebels," *International Business Times*, June 24, 2014, http://www.ibtimes.co.uk /iraq-isis-crisis-judge-who-sentenced-saddam-hussein-death -executed-by-rebels-1453975. See also Lucy Crossley, "Judge Who Sentenced Saddam Hussein to Death 'Is Captured and Executed by Isis,'" *Daily Mail*, June 22, 2014, http:// www.dailymail.co.uk/news/article-2665360/Judge-sentenced -Saddam-Hussein-death-captured-executed-ISIS.html.

37. Ibid.

38. Raymond Ibrahim, "New Islamic Caliphate Declares Jihad on . . . Muslims," *Human Events*, July 18, 2014, http:// humanevents.com/2014/07/18/new-islamic-caliphate-declares -jihad-on-muslims/.

39. Ibid.

40. Ibid.

41. Reuters, "Convert, Pay Tax, or Die, Islamic State Warns Christians," http://news.yahoo.com/convert-pay-tax-die -islamic-state-warns-christians-181415698—business.html.

42. Ibid.

43. "Tens of Thousands of Christians Flee ISIS Attack on Ninevah Town of Qaraqosh (Hamdaniya)," Yahoo! News, June 26, 2014, http://news.yahoo.com/tens-thousands -christians-flee-isis-attack-nineveh-town-212600821.html.

44. Ibid.

45. Ibid. See also Sophia Jones, "In Face of ISIS Advance, Many Iraqi Christians Insist on Staying Put," *Huffington Post*, June 25, 2014, http://www.huffingtonpost.com/2014/06/25/iraqi -christians-isis_n_5527266.html.

46. Ibid.

47. Ibid.

48. Ibid.

49. Yasmine Hafiz, "Reported ISIS Member Says They Will Destroy the Kaaba in Mecca, 'Kill Those Who Worship Stones,'" *Huffington Post*, July 1, 2014, http:// www.huffingtonpost.com/2014/07/01/isis-destroy-kaaba -mecca_n_5547635.html.

50. Ibid.

51. Sophie Jane Evans, "Shocking Moment: Isis Militants Take Sledgehammers to Mosul Tomb of Prophet Jonah as More Than 50 Blindfolded Bodies Are Found Massacred South of Baghdad," *Daily Mail*, July 9, 2014, http://www.dailymail.co .uk/news/article-2685923/Shocking-moment-ISIS-militants -sledgehammers-Mosul-tomb-Prophet-Jonah-50-blindfolded -bodies-massacred-south-Baghdad.html.

52. Ibid.

53. Frances Martel, "Sunni Mufti: ISIS and Affiliates Have Killed over 300 Sunni Imams, Preachers," Breitbart, July 3, 2014, http://www.breitbart.com/Big-Peace/2014/07/03 /Sunni-Mufti-ISIS-and-Affiliates-Have-Killed-Over-300 -Sunni-Imams-and-Preachers; "Iraq: ISIS Kidnaps Shia Turkmen, Destroys Shrines," Human Rights Watch, June 28, 2014, http://www.hrw.org/news/2014/06/27/iraq-isis -kidnaps-shia-turkmen-destroys-shrines; "Islamic State Claims Shia Mosque Destruction," Al Jazeera, July 5, 2014, http://www.aljazeera.com/news/middleeast/ 2014/07/islamic -state-claims-shia-mosque-destruction-20147414533266331 .html; "Jordan's Abu Qatada: Caliphate Declaration 'Void,'" *Daily Star Lebanon*, July 15, 2014, http://www.dailystar.com .lb/News/Middle-East/2014/Jul-15/263931-jordans-abu -qatada-caliphate-declaration-void.ashx#axzz37l9q5wZI.

54. Johnlee Varghese, "Isis Issues Threat to US with Decapitated Head, Says Calamity Will Befall the Country," *International Business Times*, June 26, 2014, http://www.ibtimes.co.in/isis -issues-threat-us-decapitated-head-says-calamity-will-befall -country-603119.

55. Ibid.

56. John Rossomando and Ravi Kumar, "Emboldened ISIS Threatens Americans," Investigative Project, June 26, 2014, http://www.investigativeproject.org/4440/emboldened-isis -threatens-americans.

57. See Dalit Halevy and Ari Yashar, "ISIS Parades Scud Missile 'Heading Towards Israel,'" *Arutz Sheva*, July 1, 2014, http:// www.israelnationalnews.com/News/News.aspx/182409# .U7RnSLGf-ik.

58. "ISIS Weighs In on Israeli-Palestinian Conflict," Yeshiva World, July 16, 2014, http://www. theyeshivaworld.com/news /headlines-breaking-stories/247816/isis-weighs-in-on-israeli -palestinian-conflict.html.

59. Ibid.

60. Ibid.

61. "New Terrorist Video Rails Against Jews," Anti-Defamation League, June 3, 2014, http://blog. adl.org/international/new -terrorist-video-rails-against-jews. Sura 1.766 mandates that Jews "[b]ecome apes—despised and disgraced!" because the Jews had "disdainfully persisted in that from which they were forbidden."

62. "ISIS Weighs In On Israeli-Palestinian Conflict."

63. "ISIS Militants Threaten to Invade, Take Over Spain," InfoWars.com, July 5, 2014, http://www.infowars.com/isis -militants-threaten-to-invade-take-over-spain/.

64. "'We'll Take Back Spain': Fighters Claim ISIS to Seize 'Occupied Lands,'" RT, July 4, 2014, http://rt.com /news/170480-spain-isis-invade-threat/.

65. Christopher Livesay, "Rome Is Not Intimidated by Isis Threats to Conquer It for the Caliphate," VICE News,

July 11, 2014, https://news.vice.com/article/rome-is-not
-intimidated-by-isis-threats-to-conquer-it-for-the-caliphate.

66. Ibid.

67. Jeremy Bender, "ISIS Militants Captured 52 American-Made
Artillery Weapons That Cost $50,000 Each," *Business Insider*,
July 15, 2014, http://www.businessinsider.com/isis-has-52
-american-weapons-that-can-hit-baghdad-2014-7. See also
Douglas Ernst, "ISIL Captured 52 U.S.-Made Howitzers;
Artillery Weapons Cost 500K Each," *Washington Times*, July
15, 2014, http://www.washingtontimes.com/news/2014/jul/15
/isil-captured-52-us-made-howitzers-artillery-weapo/.

68. Ibid.

69. Bender, "ISIS Militants Captured 52 American-Made
Artillery Weapons That Cost $50,000 Each."

70. Bill Gertz, "ISIL Moving Seized U.S. Tanks, Humvees to
Syria," *Washington Free Beacon*, June 17, 2014.

71. Perry Chiaramonte, "Stolen Uranium Compounds Not Only
Dirty Bomb Ingredients Within ISIS' Grasp, Say Experts,"
Fox News, July 15, 2014, http://www.foxnews.com
/world/2014/07/15/stolen-uranium-compounds-not-only
-dirty-bomb-ingredients-within-isis-grasp/.

72. Ibid.

73. Ibid.

74. Bill Hutchinson, "ISIS Seizes Chemical Weapons Depot Near
Baghdad, May Have Access to Deadly Sarin Gas Rockets,"
New York *Daily News*, July 9, 2014.

CHAPTER FOUR. HAMAS: ARCHITECTS OF ETERNAL JIHAD

1. https://www.youtube.com/watch?v=uAx6bLkVcgw.

2. Jonathan Masters, "Hamas," Council on Foreign Relations,
November 24, 2012, http://www.cfr.org/israel/hamas/p8968.

3. "Palestine Liberation Organization," palestineun.org,
http://palestineun.org/about-palestine/palestine-liberation
-organization/.

4. Masters, "Hamas."

5. *Hamas*, whose name is an acronym for *Harakat al-Muqawana al-Islamiya*, which translates to "Islamic Resistance Movement," is the "largest and most influential Palestinian militant movement." Masters, "Hamas."

6. See Covenant of the Islamic Resistance Movement—Hamas, art. 2 (1988) (hereinafter Charter), stating that "the Islamic Resistance Movement is one of the wings of the Muslim Brotherhood in Palestine," http://www.memri.org/report/en/0/0/0/0/0/0/50/1609.htm.

7. The last Palestinian presidential election took place in 2005. Hugh Naylor, "Palestinian Elections Delayed by Fatah-Hamas Bickering," *National*, March 9, 2012, http://www.thenational.ae/news/world/palestinian-elections-delayed-by-hamas-fatah-bickering.

8. "Abbas Achieves Landslide Poll Win," BBC News, January 10, 2005, http://news.bbc.co.uk/2/hi/ middle_east/4160171.stm.

9. Naylor, "Palestinian Elections Delayed by Fatah-Hamas Bickering."

10. Ibid.

11. Donald Macintyre, "The State of Gaza: Five Years After Hamas Took Power in the City, How Has Life Changed for Its Citizens?," *Independent*, June 10, 2012, http://www.independent.co.uk/news/world/middle-east/the-state-of-gaza-five-years-after-hamas-took-power-in-the-city-how-has-life-changed-for-its-citizens7831408.html.

12. "Gaza E.R.: Fatah vs. Hamas," PBS, August 14, 2007, http://www.pbs.org/wnet/wideangle/episodes/gaza-e-r/fatah-vs-hamas/1227/.

13. Charter, arts. 7, 12, 13.

14. Ibid.

15. US Department of State, Foreign Terrorist Organizations, http://www.state.gov/j/ct/rls/other/des/123085.htm, accessed July 15, 2014; Masters, "Hamas"; "EU Blacklists Hamas Political Wing," BBC News, September 11, 2003, http://news.bbc.co.uk/2/hi/middle_east/3100518.stm.

16. Charter, art. 1.

17. "Intifada is an Arabic word for 'civil uprising' that literally means 'shaking off.'" "The First Intifada," *Ma'an News,* August 16, 2009, http://www.maannews.net/eng/ViewDetails .aspx?ID=212093.

18. Charter, art. 6.

19. Masters, "Hamas."

20. Ibid.

21. Charter, quoting the Quran (3:110–112).

22. Ibid., arts. 5, 8.

23. Ibid., introduction, quoting Hasan al-Banna, founder of the Muslim Brotherhood in 1928 and director general until his assassination in 1949.

24. Ibid., art. 14. Quran 17:1 states: "Glory to (Allah) Who did take His Servant For a Journey by night From the Sacred Mosque To the Farthest Mosque, Whose precincts We did Bless—in order that We Might show him some Of Our Signs: for He Is the One Who heareth And seeth (all things)." Ali, *The Meaning of the Holy Qur'an,* 17:1. Nocturnal journey is a reference to Muhammad's "Night Journey" from the "sacred mosque" (the Ka'aba in Mecca) to "the Farthest Mosque" (which Muslims consider to be a reference to the al-Aqsa mosque in Jerusalem). In his commentary on verse 17:1, Abdullah Yusuf Ali, a notable translator of and commentator on the Quran, states that during the night journey, "[t]he Holy Prophet [Muhammad] was first transported to the seat of the earlier revelations [Torah, Psalms, the Gospels] in Jerusalem, and then taken through the seven heavens even to the Sublime Throne, and initiated into the spiritual mysteries of the human soul struggling in Space and Time." Ibid. Note that the word *aqsa* means farthest and does not necessarily mean that Muhammad was actually referring to the site of the Jewish Temple in Jerusalem. Furthermore, this verse does not mention the word Jerusalem or make any reference to it. Muslims, however, believe the farthest mosque is the reference to the Dome of the Rock on the Temple Mount in Jerusalem. One hadith observes Muhammad as saying "[w]hen the people

of Quraish did not believe me (i.e. the story of my Night Journey), I stood up in Al-Hijr and Allah displayed Jerusalem in front of me, and I began describing it to them while I was looking at it.'" Sahih Bukhari, Vol. 5, Bk. 58, No. 226, http://sahih-bukhari.com/Pages/Bukhari_5_58.php.

25. Charter, art. 11.
26. Ibid., art. 7.
27. Ibid., art. 3.
28. Ibid., art. 6.
29. Ibid., art. 6.
30. Ibid., art. 13.
31. Ibid.
32. Ibid., preamble.
33. Ibid.
34. Ibid., art. 13.
35. See text accompanying notes 194–206.
36. U.S. Department of State, Country Reports on Terrorism 2011, ch. 6, "Foreign Terrorist Organizations," Office of the Coordinator for Counterterrorism, July 31, 2012, http://www.state.gov/j/ct/rls/crt/2011/195553.htm.
37. Masters, "Hamas."
38. U.S. Department of State, Country Reports on Terrorism 2011: "Designated as a Foreign Terrorist Organization on October 8, 1997, Hamas possesses military and political wings and came into being in late 1987 at the onset of the first Palestinian uprising, or Intifada, as an outgrowth of the Palestinian branch of the Muslim Brotherhood."
39. Council Common Position 2003/651/CFSP of 12 September 2003 updating Common Position 2001/931/CFSP on the application of specific measures to combat terrorism and repealing Common Position 2003/482/CFSP, http://eur-lex.europa.eu/LexUriServ/LexUriServ.do?uri=CELEX:32003E0651:EN:HTML, listing "Hamas (including Hamas-Izz al-Din al-Qassem)" among "Groups and Entities" defined as terrorist organizations. See also Anton La Guardia, "Hamas Is Added to EUs Blacklist of

Terror," *Telegraph*, September 12, 2003, http://www.telegraph
.co.uk/ news/worldnews/middleeast/israel/1441311/Hamas
-is-added-to-EUs-blacklist-of-terror.html.

40. Ibid.
41. U.S. Department of State, Country Reports on Terrorism
2011.
42. Masters, "Hamas."
43. Ibid.
44. Fares Akram and Jodi Rudoren, "To Shape Young
Palestinians, Hamas Creates Its Own Textbooks," *New
York Times*, November 3, 2013, http://www.nytimes
.com/2013/11/04/world/middleeast/to-shape-young
-palestinians-hamas-creates-its-own-textbooks.html?page
wanted=all&_r=0.
45. U.S. Department of State, Country Reports on Terrorism
2011.
46. Marissa Newman, "Hamas Said to Have Executed Dozens of
Tunnel Diggers," *Times of Israel*, August 11, 2014, http://www
.timesofisrael.com/hamas-said-to-have-executed-dozens-of
-tunnel-diggers/.
47. "Gaza E.R.: Fatah vs. Hamas," PBS. See also "Profile: Fatah
Palestinian Movement," BBC News, August 4, 2009, http://
news.bbc.co.uk/ 2/hi/middle_east/1371998.stm.
48. FATEH Constitution, arts. 2, 17, http://www.acpr.org.il
/resources/fatehconstitution.html; see also PLO Charter,
arts. 3, 9 (1968), http://www.iris.org.il/plochart.htm.
49. "Gaza E.R.: Fatah vs. Hamas," PBS.
50. FATEH Constitution, arts. 7, 8; see also PLO Charter,
arts. 15, 22.
51. "Gaza E.R.: Fatah vs. Hamas," PBS.
52. Andrew Higgins, "How Israel Helped to Spawn Hamas," *Wall
Street Journal*, January 24, 2009, http://online.wsj.com/news
/articles/SB123275572295011847.
53. Charter, art. 27.
54. Ben Lynfield, "Make Way, Fatah Young Guns Tell Arafat
Generation," *Independent*, August 4, 2009, http://www

.independent.co.uk/news/world/middle-east/make-way-fatah
-young-guns-tell-arafat-generation-1766950.html. See also
"Profile: Fatah."

55. "Gaza E.R.: Fatah vs. Hamas," PBS. See also Lynfield, "Make
Way."

56. Masters, "Hamas." See also Richard Falk, "Preparing the
Path to a Just Peace for Palestine/Israel," *Foreign Policy
Journal,* June 17, 2014, http://www.foreignpolicyjournal
.com/2014/06/17/preparing-the-path-to-a-just-peace-for
-palestineisrael/.

CHAPTER FIVE. HAMAS: ISRAEL'S MOST RELENTLESS ENEMY

1. Masters, "Hamas"; *see also* Bryony Jones, "Q&A: What Is
Hamas?," CNN, November 24, 2012, http://edition.cnn
.com/2012/11/16/world/meast/hamas-explainer/index.html.

2. Jones, "Q&A: What Is Hamas?"

3. The International Crisis Group is "an independent, non-
profit, non-governmental organisation committed to
preventing and resolving deadly conflict." Its staff publishes
reports and briefings that give policy recommendations
regarding "over 50 conflict and potential conflict situations"
that are monitored by its field agents. "About Crisis Group,"
International Crisis Group, http://www.crisisgroup.org/en
/about.aspx.

4. Jones, "Q&A: What Is Hamas?"

5. Masters, "Hamas."

6. Jim Zanotti, "Hamas: Background and Issues for Congress,"
Congressional Research Service, December 2, 2010, http://
www.fas.org/sgp/crs/mideast/R41514.pdf.

7. Sara Sidner, "First Rocket Fired from Gaza into Israel Since
November Cease-fire," CNN, February 26, 2013, http://
edition.cnn.com/2013/02/26/world/meast/israel-gaza-rocket
/index.html. See also "Calm Elusive as Rockets Rain in
Gaza, Israel," CNN, November 21, 2012, http://edition.cnn
.com/2012/11/20/world/meast/gaza-israel-strike/index.html

(Hamas repeating its refusal to recognize Israel's right to
exist).
8. "Israel Blames Hamas for All Attacks from Gaza," Al
Jazeera, December 27, 2013, http://www.aljazeera.com/news
/middleeast/2013/12/israel-blames-hamas-all-attacks-from
-gaza-201312270847706182.html.
9. Hamas carried out its first suicide bombing in April 1993,
and only months later, Hamas publicly condemned the Oslo
Accords, an historic pact that had been agreed to by both
Israel and the PLO. Masters, "Hamas." Hamas claimed
responsibility for its first suicide bombing directed at Israeli
civilians on April 6, 1994. The bomber in Afula killed 8
civilians and wounded 34. Joe Stork, *Erased in a Moment:
Suicide Bombing Attacks Against Israeli Civilians* (New York:
Human Rights Watch, 2002), 66. Only one week later, Hamas
claimed responsibility for a suicide bombing on a crowded
bus, an attack that killed 5 Israeli civilians and wounded
30 others. Clyde Haberman, "5 Killed in Israel as Second
Bomber Blows Up a Bus," *New York Times*, April 14, 1994,
http://www.nytimes.com/1994/04/14/world/5-killed-in
-israel-as-second-bomber-blows-up-a-bus.html. On October
19, 1994, a Hamas suicide bomber detonated a bomb while
on an Israeli passenger bus in Tel Aviv, killing 22 civilians
and wounding another 48. "One Victim Survives Her 2d Bus
Bombing," *New York Times*, July 25, 1995, http://www.nytimes
.com/1995/07/25/world/one-victim-survives-her-2d-bus
-bombing.html. Another Hamas suicide attack on an Israeli
bus happened on April 9, 1995, when the attacker rammed
his bomb-rigged car into the bus, causing an explosion
that killed 8 and injured 52. Elaine Ruth Fletcher, "Terror
Deals a Blow to Mideast Peace," *SFGate*, April 10, 1995,
http://www.sfgate.com/news/article/Terror-deals-a-blow-to
-Mideast-peace-3148607.php. On July 30, 1997, two Hamas
suicide bombers detonated bombs in a Jerusalem open-air
market, killing 14 civilians and wounding another 150. "14

Killed in Jerusalem Suicide Bombings," CNN, July 30, 1997, http://www.cnn.com/WORLD/9707/30/jerusalem.noon/. On September 4, 1997, three Hamas bombers detonated nail bombs on Ben Yehuda Street, a crowded Jerusalem thoroughfare, killing 8 and injuring over 150 others. "1997: Suicide Bombings Put Peace Visit in Doubt," BBC News, September 4, 1997, http://news.bbc.co.uk/ onthisday/hi /dates/stories/september/4/newsid_2499000/2499009.stm. On June 1, 2001, a suicide bomber detonated his bomb outside a Tel Aviv discotheque, killing 21 teenagers and wounding 120 others. "Tel-Aviv Suicide Bombing at the Dolphin Disco," Israel Ministry of Foreign Affairs, June 2, 2001, http://mfa.gov.il/MFA/MFA-Archive/2001/Pages/Tel -Aviv%20suicide%20bombing%20at%20the%20v Dolphin %20disco%20-%201-.aspx. A Hamas suicide bomber killed 15 Israelis inside a Jerusalem restaurant, including an Israeli family with three children, provoking mourners to call Hamas's campaign of violence "a Holocaust." " 'This Isn't a Funeral. It's a Holocaust,' " *Guardian*, August 10, 2001, http:// www.theguardian.com/world/2001/aug/11/israel. A series of suicide bombings, including another bombing at the Ben Yehuda Street pedestrian mall, over the weekend of December 1, 2001, killed 25 people and wounded over 200. "Bomb Blasts Kill Scores in Israel," Fox News, December 2, 2001, http://www.foxnews.com/story/ 2001/12/02/bomb-blasts -kill-scores-in-israel/. A suicide bombing carried out by the Izz al-Din al-Qassem Brigades killed 11 people and injured 54 at a Jerusalem café. Suzanne Goldenberg, "Bombing Shatters Illusions in an Oasis of Civility," *Guardian*, March 10, 2002, http://www.theguardian.com/world/2002/mar/11 /israel1. A May 2002 Hamas suicide bombing at a billiards hall in Rishon LeZion killed 15 and injured another 60. Matthew Kalman, "Israel Vows to Hit Back After Suicide Bomb Kills 15," *Daily Mail*, http://www.dailymail.co.uk/news /article-113414/Israel-vows-hit-suicide-bomb-kills-15.html. Hamas claimed responsibility for using a bomb packed with ball bearings in a suicide attack on June 18, 2002, that killed 19 bus passengers, including an eleven-year-old girl. James Bennet, "Suicide Bomber Hits Jerusalem Bus, Killing at Least 18," *New York Times*, June 19, 2002, http://www.nytimes.com /learning/teachers/featured_articles/20020619wednesday .html. On September 29, 2004, a Hamas militant fired a Qassam rocket into Israel, killing two children, ages 4 and 2. "Israel Kills Hamas Militant Blamed for Deadly Rocket Attack," *Los Angeles Times*, October 10, 2004, http://articles .latimes.com/2004/oct/10/world/fg-gaza10. Hamas launched an antiaircraft missile at an Israeli school bus moments after it had dropped off most of the students. The one remaining passenger, sixteen-year-old Daniel Viflic, died in the explosion. "Boy Hurt in Gaza Rocket Attack on Israeli Bus Dies of His Wounds," *Haaretz*, April 17, 2011, http://www .haaretz.com/news/ diplomacy-defense/boy-hurt-in-gaza -rocket-attack-on-israeli-bus-dies-of-his-wounds-1.356477. See also Foreign Secretary Statement on the Death of Daniel Viflic, Foreign and Commonwealth Office, April 17, 2011, https://www.gov.uk/government/news/foreign-secretary -statement-on-the-death-of-daniel-viflic.

10. Masters, "Hamas," citing "Rocket Attacks on Israel from Gaza," Israel Defense Forces, http:// www.idfblog.com/facts -figures/rocket-attacks-toward-israel/.

11. Serge Schmemann, "Bombing in Israel: The Overview; 4th Terror Blast in Israel Kills 14 at Mall in Tel Aviv; Nine-Day Toll Grows to 61," N.Y. Times (5 Mar. 1996), http://www.nytimes.com/1996/03/05/world/bombing -israel-overview-4th-terror-blast-israel-kills-14-mall-tel -aviv-nine-day.html?scp=1&sq=dizengoff%20center%20 suicide&st=cse&pagewanted=print.

12. "Alleged Passover Massacre Plotter Arrested," CNN, March 26, 2008, http://edition.cnn.com/2008/ WORLD /meast/03/26/israel.hamas/.

13. Conal Urquhart, "Israel Attacks Gaza as Bus Bomb Kills 15," *Guardian*, March 6, 2003, http://www.theguardian.com

/world/2003/mar/06/israel; "Suicide Blast Hits Jerusalem Bus," BBC News, June 11, 2003, http://news.bbc.co.uk/2 /hi/2982068.stm; James Bennet, "Bombing Kills 18 and Hurts Scores on Jerusalem Bus," *New York Times*, August 20, 2003, http://www.nytimes.com/2003/08/20/world/bombing-kills -18-and-hurts-scores-on-jerusalem-bus.html.

CHAPTER SIX. HAMAS CREATES A UNITY GOVERNMENT WITH FATAH, THEN LAUNCHES WAR

1. Tzippe Barrow, "Hamas, Fatah Post Facebook Threats," CBN News, June 11, 2014, http://www.cbn.com/cbnnews /insideisrael/2014/July/Hamas-Fatah-Post-Facebook-Threats/.

2. Lesley Wroughton and Patricia Zengerle, "Obama Administration to Work with Palestinian Unity Government," Reuters, June 2, 2014, http://www.reuters.com /article/2014/06/03/us-palestinian-unity-usa-idUSKB N0ED1VQ20140603.

3. See 18 U.S.C. Sections 2339A and 2339B.

4. Ibid.

5. "Kidnapped Israeli Teenagers Shot 10 Times with Silenced Gun—US Investigators," RT, July 9, 2014, http://rt.com /news/171652-israeli-teenagers-shot-investigation/. See also Karl Vick, "Israel Holds Breath Over Three Teens Kidnapped on West Bank," *Time*, June 17, 2014, http://time.com/2885286 /israel-kidnap-naftali-fraenkel-gilad-shaar-eyal-yifrach/; Isabel Kershner, "Palestinian Leader Pledges to Hold Abductors of Israeli Teenagers to Account," *New York Times*, June 18, 2014, http://www.nytimes.com/2014/06/19/world /middleeast/ palestinian-leader-condemns-kidnapping-of -israeli-teenagers.html.

6. Ibid.

7. Sharona Schwartz, "This Is How Some Palestinians Are Celebrating the Kidnapping of Three Israeli Teens," *Blaze*, June 15, 2014, http://www.theblaze.com/stories/2014/06/15 /this-is-how-some-palestinians-are-celebrating-a-kidnapping/.

8. Ibid.

9. "PM to Kerry: Feared Abductions a Result of Hamas Entry into Government," *Times of Israel*, June 13, 2014, http://www .timesofisrael.com/livni-urges-kerry-to-help-locate-missing -teens/.

10. William Booth and Ruth Eglash, "Israel Presses Gaza Assault as Hamas Rockets Fly; Netanyahu Rules Out Cease-fire," *Washington Post*, July 10, 2014, http://www.washingtonpost .com/world/israel-pounds-gaza-for-third-straight-day-while -hamas-fires-rockets-at-israeli-towns/2014/07/10/902d4896 -ab00-47f0-bd53-01040c16379e_story.html.

11. Ibid.

12. Convention (IV) Relative to the Protection of Civilian Persons in Time of War, art. 3, August 12, 1949, 6 U.S.T. 3316, 75 U.N.T.S. 135.

13. Booth and Eglash, "Israel Presses Gaza Assault as Hamas Rockets Fly."

CHAPTER EIGHT. THE 2014 GAZA WAR: WHO ARE THE REAL WAR CRIMINALS?

1. "Murdered Israeli Teens Mourned in Joint Funeral, As Israel Launches Strike Against Hamas," Fox News, July 1, 2014, http://www.foxnews.com/world/2014/07/01/israeli-teens -found-dead/.

2. Lea Speyer, "360 Arrested As Operation Brothers Keeper Enters 12th Day," *Breaking Israel News*, June 24, 2014, http://www.breakingisraelnews.com/17063/269 -terrorists-arrested-operation-brothers-keeper-enters-12th -day/#kswx537rQzX62L97.97.

3. Ibid.; see also "Murdered Israeli Teens Mourned."

4. Ari Soffer, "Watch: Hamas Official Heaps Praise on 'Heroic' Kidnap Operation," *Arutz Sheva*, June 18, 2014, http://www .israelnationalnews.com/News/News.aspx/181891#.U8 _wQLGf-ik.

5. "Israeli Air Strikes Hit Targets in Gaza," Al Jazeera, June 29,

2014, http://www.aljazeera. com/news/middleeast/2014/06 /israeli-airstrikes-attack-targets-gaza-201462984832208983 .html.

6. Ibid.

7. Ben Wedeman and Dana Ford, "Missing Israeli Teens Found Dead in West Bank," CNN, June 30, 2014, http://www.cnn .com/2014/06/30/world/meast/israel-missing-teenagers/.

8. Ibid.

9. Dan Kedmey, "Israel Hammers Gaza Strip over Kidnapped Teens' Deaths," *Time*, July 1, 2014, http://time.com/2944876 /israel-hammers-gaza-strip-over-kidnapped-teens-deaths/.

10. Marcy Kreiter, "Israel Mounts Operation to End Gaza Rocket Fire," *International Business Times*, July 7, 2014, http://www .ibtimes.com/israel-mounts-operation-end-gaza-rocket-fire -1621462.

11. See, e.g., U.N. Charter, art. 2(4): "All Members shall refrain in their international relations from the threat or use of force against the territorial integrity or political independence of any state, or in any other manner inconsistent with the Purposes of the United Nations."

12. U.N. Charter, art. 51.

13. David B. Rivkin et al., "Preemption and Law in the Twenty-First Century," 5 *Chicago Journal of International Law* 467, 476 (2005).

14. See, e.g., Armed Activities on the Territory of the Congo (Dem. Rep. Congo. v. Uganda), 2005 I.C.J. ¶ 11 (17 Dec.) (separate opinion of Judge Simma), http://www.icj-cij.org /docket/files/116/10467.pdf.

15. Sean D. Murphy, *Principles of International Law* (St. Paul, MN: Thomson/West, 2006), 447 (emphasis added).

16. Rosalyn Higgins, *Problems and Process: International Law and How We Use It* (New York: Oxford University Press, 1995), 232; see also Christopher Greenwood, *Essays on War in International Law* (London: Cameron May, 2006), 80.

17. Harriet Sherwood, "Gaza Crisis: How the Game Has Changed Since Egypt's Tabling of Ceasefire Plan," *Guardian*,

July 21, 2014, http://www.theguardian.com/world/2014
/jul/21/gaza-crisis-how-game-changed-since-egypt-tabling
-ceasefire-plan.

18. Jodi Rudoren and Anne Barnard, "Israeli Military Invades
Gaza, with Sights Set on Hamas Operations," *New York Times*,
July 17, 2014, http://nyti.ms/1nA2HQS.

19. Heather Saul, "Israel-Hamas 72-Hour Ceasefire Crumbles
As Dozens Killed in Gaza Shelling," *Independent*, August
1, 2014, http://www.independent.co.uk/news/world/middle
-east/israelgaza-conflict-kerry-warns-72hour-unconditional
-ceasefire-is-a-respite-not-an-end-9641781.html.

20. "U.S. Calls Hamas Attack 'Barbaric' Violation of Gaza
Ceasefire: CNN," Reuters, August 1, 2014, http://www
.reuters.com/article/2014/08/01/us-mideast-gaza-whitehouse
-idUSKBN0G143S20140801.

21. ICRC, Protocol Additional to the Geneva Conventions
of 12 August 1949, and relating to the Protection of Victims
of International Armed Conflicts (Protocol I), art. 52,
8 June 1977, 1125 UNTS 3 (herein after referred to as
Protocol I).

22. Ibid. (emphasis added).

23. Ibid., art. 28.

24. ICRC, Commentary on the Additional Protocols of 8 June
1977 to the Geneva Conventions of 12 August 1949, ¶ 1953,
at 620–21 (1987) (emphasis added), http://www.loc.gov/rr
/frd/Military_Law/pdf/Commentary_GC_Protocols.pdf.

25. Jean-Marie Henckaerts and Louise Doswald-Beck,
International Committee of the Red Cross, Customary
International Humanitarian Law: Practice ¶¶ 328–29, 332,
334, 336–37, 339, at 184–85 (2005).

26. Ibid. ¶¶ 329, 331, 336, 339, at 184–85.

27. Stefan Oeter, "Methods and Means of Combat," in Dieter
Fleck, ed., *The Handbook of International Humanitarian Law*,
2nd ed. 119, 135 (New York: Oxford University Press, 2008),
119, 135.

28. http://acdemocracy.org/wp-content/uploads/2014/08/Hamas

-Urban-Warfare-Tactics.pdf?utm_source=Hamas+Urban
+Warfare+Tactics&utm_campaign=Hamas+Urban+Warfare
+Tactics&utm_medium=email.
29. UN General Assembly, Rome Statute of the International
Criminal Court (last amended 2010), art. 8(2)(b)(ii), 17 July
1998 (hereinafter Rome Statute).

CHAPTER NINE. HAMAS SYSTEMATICALLY AND INTENTIONALLY VIOLATED THE LAW OF WAR

1. Protocol I, art. 58(a). Although Israel is not bound by
Additional Protocol I as a matter of treaty obligation, Israel
recognizes that the protocol reflects customary international
law. Israel Ministry of Foreign Affairs, *Operation in Gaza:
Factual and Legal Aspects* (Jerusalem: State of Israel, 2008), 38.
2. Customary International Humanitarian Law, Rule 23,
Location of Military Objectives outside Densely Populated
Areas, ICRC, http://www.icrc.org/customary-ihl/eng/print
/v1_cha_chapter6_rule23.
3. Israel-Lebanon Ceasefire Understanding, art. 3 (1996).
4. Protocol I, art. 51(7).
5. Convention (IV) relative to the Protection of Civilian Persons
in Time of War, art. 28, 12 August 1949.
6. Rome Statute, art. 8(2)(b)(xxiii).
7. Customary International Humanitarian Law, Rule 97, Human
Shields, ICRC, http://www.icrc.org/ customary-ihl/eng/docs
/v1_cha_chapter32_rule97.
8. Protocol I, art. 48.
9. ICRC, "Civilian and Medical Workers Pay Price of Conflict,"
July 10, 2014, http://www.icrc.org/eng/resources/documents
/news-release/2014/israel-palestine-gaza-civilian-medical.htm.
10. Anne Barnard and Jodi Rudoren, "Israel Says That Hamas
Uses Civilian Shields, Reviving Debate," *New York Times*, July
23, 2014, http://www.nytimes.com/2014/07/24/world
/middleeast/israel-says-hamas-is-using-civilians-as-shields
-in-gaza.html (emphases added).

11. Ibid.
12. Protocol I, art. 16.
13. Ibid.
14. http://acdemocracy.org/wp-content/uploads/2014/08/Hamas
    -Urban-Warfare-Tactics.pdf?utm_source=Hamas+Urban
    +Warfare+Tactics&utm_campaign=Hamas+Urban+Warfare
    +Tactics&utm_medium=email.
15. Barnard, and Rudoren, Rudoren, "Israel Says That Hamas
    Uses Civilian Shields, Reviving Debate."
16. "Gaza Conflict: Fighting intensifies in town of Khan Younis,"
    Associated Press, July 23, 2014.
17. Barnard and Rudoren, "Israel Says That Hamas Uses Civilian
    Shields, Reviving Debate."
18. "Rockets Found at UN Gaza School Went Missing,"
    Washington Post, July 23, 2014, http://www.washingtonpost
    .com/world/middle_east/rockets-found-at-un-gaza-school
    -have-gone-missing/2014/07/23/e1f7e206-12c7-11e4-ac56
    -773e54a65906_story.html. See also "UNRWA Strongly
    Condemns Placement of Rockets in School," UNRWA, July
    17, 2014, http://www.unrwa.org/newsroom/press-releases
    /unrwa-strongly-condemns-placement-rockets-school.
19. "Rockets Found at UN Gaza School Went Missing."
20. Ibid.; see also "UNRWA Condemns Placement of Rockets,
    for a Second Time, in One of Its Schools," UNRWA, July 22,
    2014, http://www.unrwa.org/newsroom/press-releases/unrwa
    -condemns-placement-rockets-second-time-one-its-schools.
21. "Rockets Found at UN Gaza School Went Missing."
22. Josh Levs et al., "Deaths Mount in Gaza and Israel as U.S.
    Pushes Cease-Fire," CNN, July 22, 2014, http://www.cnn
    .com/2014/07/21/world/meast/mideast-crisis/.
23. "Rockets Found at UN Gaza School Went Missing."
24. http://acdemocracy.org/wp-content/uploads/2014/08/Hamas
    -Urban-Warfare-Tactics.pdf?utm_source=Hamas+Urban
    +Warfare+Tactics&utm_campaign=Hamas+Urban
    +Warfare+Tactics&utm_medium=email

25. "The Price of Hamas' Underground Terror Network," IDF Blog, July 26, 2014, http://www.idfblog.com/blog/2014/07/26/price-hamas-underground-terror-network/.
26. Levs, "Deaths Mount in Gaza and Israel."
27. "The Price of Hamas' Underground Terror Network."
28. "Shuja'iya: Hamas' Terror Fortress in Gaza," Israel Defense Forces, July 20, 2014, http://www.idfblog.com/blog/2014/07/20/shujaiya-hamas-terror-fortress-gaza/.
29. Ibid.
30. Convention (IV) relative to the Protection of Civilian Persons in Time of War, art. 28, 12 August 1949.
31. See Rome Statute, art. 8(2)(b)(xxiii) and accompanying text.
32. http://acdemocracy.org/wp-content/uploads/2014/08/Hamas-Urban-Warfare-Tactics.pdf?utm_source=Hamas+Urban+Warfare+Tactics&utm_campaign=Hamas+Urban+Warfare+Tactics&utm_medium=email.
33. Ibid.
34. "Israel Bombs Gaza's Only Rehab Hospital: Staff Forced to Evacuate Paralyzed Patients After Shelling," Democracy Now, July 18, 2014, http://www.democracynow.org/2014/7/18/israel_bombs_gazas_only_rehab_hospital.
35. Stuart Winer, "WATCH: IDF Targets Hospital Used as Hamas Command Center," *Times of Israel*, July 23, 2014, http://www.timesofisrael.com/idf-targets-hospital-hamas-used-as-firing-position/.
36. "Israel Bombs Gaza's Only Rehab Hospital."
37. Ibid.
38. Ibid.
39. Commentary on the Additional Protocols.
40. http://acdemocracy.org/wp-content/uploads/2014/08/Hamas-Urban-Warfare-Tactics.pdf?utm_source=Hamas+Urban+Warfare+Tactics&utm_campaign=Hamas+Urban+Warfare+Tactics&utm_medium=email.
41. Protocol I, art. 52.
42. See id., art. 51(4).

43. Ibid.
44. Ibid., art. 51(5)(b) (emphasis added).
45. Karen Yourish and Josh Keller, "The Toll in Gaza and Israel, Day by Day," *New York Times*, August 8, 2014, http://www .nytimes.com/interactive/2014/07/15/world/middleeast/toll -israel-gaza-conflict.html.
46. "Hamas Launches Rockets on Civilians in Gaza," IDF Blog, July 31, 2014, http://www.idfblog.com/blog/2014/07/31 /hamas-launches-rockets-civilians-gaza/.
47. Protocol I, art. 51(4)(b).
48. Steven Emerson, "Hamas Claims Rockets Only Target Jews," *Algemeiner*, July 28, 2014, http://www.algemeiner .com/2014/07/28/hamas-claims-rockets-only-target-jews/.

CHAPTER TEN. THE STAKES COULD NOT BE HIGHER
1. https://www.icrc.org/eng/resources/documents /statement/2014/07-29-gaza-stop-the-killing.htm.
2. Ian Black, "U.N. Human Rights Body to Investigate Claims of Israeli Violations in Gaza," *Guardian*, July 23, 2014, http://www.theguardian.com/global/2014/jul/23/un-high -commissioner-navi-pillay-war-crimes-israel.
3. See Editorial Board, "The U.S. Should Push for the Disarming of Hamas in Gaza-Israel Cease-Fire," *Washington Post*, July 23, 2014, http://www.washingtonpost.com/opinions /the-us-should-push-for-the-disarming-of-hamas-in-gaza -israel-cease-fire/2014/07/23/7c2d1d9e-1284-11e4-8936 -26932bcfd6ed_story.html (estimating the cost of each tunnel that Hamas has dug to be roughly one million dollars).
4. See Elad Benari, "Watch: Hamas Spokesman Encourages Using Civilians as Shields," *Artuz Sheva*, July 7, 2014, http:// www.israelnationalnews.com/News/News.aspx/182729# .U9kmg7Gf-ik (reporting a video of Hamas spokesman Sami Abu Zuhri explicitly encouraging Palestinians to adopt the strategy of becoming human shields and lauding its effectiveness and its display of the brave character of Palestinians).

CHAPTER ELEVEN. OPPOSE, DON'T APPEASE: THE WAY FORWARD AGAINST JIHAD

1. David French, "First They Came for the Jews," *Patheos*, February 7, 2011.
2. Ibid.
3. Elliott Abrams, "Yasser Arafat International Airport," Council on Foreign Relations, August 8, 2014.
4. Dexter Filkins, "What We Left Behind," *New Yorker*, April 28, 2014.
5. Rosie Gray, "Obama Authorizes Strikes Against Islamic State Fighters in Iraq," *BuzzFeed*, August 7, 2014.
6. Bing West, *The Strongest Tribe: War, Politics, and the Endgame in Iraq* (New York: Random House, 2009).

The quote from Canon Andrew White, known as the vicar of Baghdad, that appears on the back cover cites as follows: www.cbn.com/cbnnews/world/2014/September/Iraq-Crisis -Worst-Persecution-Since-Holocaust/

CHAPTER TWELVE. NEW UPDATE: ISIS IS EXPANDING

1. *See*, David French, "Backing Bill Maher: Understanding the Pyramid of Support for Jihad," *National Review* (January 12, 2015) (located at: http://www.nationalreview.com/corner /411468/backing-bill-maher-understanding-pyramid-support -jihad-david-french); see also, David French, "When Barbarism Is Propaganda," *National Review* (January 7, 2015) (located at: http://www.nationalreview.com/corner/395881 /when-barbarism-propaganda-david-french).
2. "ISIS Releases Video Purporting to Show Jordanian Pilot Being Burned Alive," *Jerusalem Post* (February 3, 2015) (located at: http://www.jpost.com/Middle-East/ISIS-releases -pictures-purporting-to-show-Jordanian-pilot-being-burned -alive-389880).
3. Lizzie Dearden, "Fox News shows uncut Isis video footage of the Jordanian pilot Muath al-Kasaesbeh being burned alive," *Independent* (February 4, 2015) (located at: http://www

.independent.co.uk/news/world/middle-east/muath
-alkasaesbeh-fox-news-shows-uncut-isis-video-of-jordanian
-pilot-being-burned-alive-10023746.html).

4. Leah Barkoukis, "DHS Secretary Explains Why Obama
Won't Say 'Radical Islam' or 'Islamic Extremism,'" Townhall
.com (February 22, 2015) (located at: http://townhall.com
/tipsheet/leahbarkoukis/2015/02/22/dhs-secretary-explains
-why-obama-wont-use-term-radical-islam-n1960743).

5. The full text of the proposed authorization can be read here:
https://www.whitehouse.gov/sites/default/files/docs/aumf
_02112015.pdf.

6. See Graeme Wood, "What ISIS Really Wants," *Atlantic*
(March 2015) (located at: http://www.theatlantic.com/features
/archive/2015/02/what-isis-really-wants/384980/).

7. Burak Bekdil, "Hamas in Turkey: 'Humanitarian Activity,'"
Gatestone Institute (March 6, 2015) (located at: http://www
.gatestoneinstitute.org/5324/hamas-turkey).

8. Mel Robbins, "Call Oklahoma beheading what it is:
Terrorism," CNN (September 30, 2014) (located at: http://
www.cnn.com/2014/09/30/opinion/robbins-oklahoma
-nolen/).

9. Joshua Keating, "Is This the ISIS Backlash We've Been
Waiting For?" *Slate* (October 23, 2014) (located at: http://www
.slate.com/blogs/the_world_/2014/10/23/ottawa_shooting_is
_this_the_isis_backlash_we_ve_been_waiting_for.html).

10. Michael Pearson, Jethro Mullen, and Anna Coren, "With
two hostages and gunmen dead, grim investigation starts in
Sydney," CNN (December 15, 2014) (located at: http://www
.cnn.com/2014/12/15/world/asia/australia-sydney-hostage
-situation/).

11. "Obama ignites social media by calling Paris kosher deli
attack 'random,'" *Jerusalem Post* (February 11, 2015) (located at:
http://www.jpost.com/International/Obama-lights-up-social
-media-by-calling-Paris-kosher-deli-attack-random-390662).

12. Chris Hughes, "Charlie Hebdo massacre predicted in
tweets: did ISIS plot Paris terror attacks?" *Daily Mirror*

(January 8, 2015) (located at: http://www.mirror.co.uk/news /world-news/charlie-hebdo-massacre-predicted -tweets-4945471).

13. Ralph Ellis, Holly Yan, and Susanne Gargiulo, "Denmark terror suspect swore fidelity to ISIS leader on Facebook page," CNN (February 23, 2015) (located at: http://www.cnn.com /2015/02/16/europe/denmark-shootings/).

14. "ISIS video appears to show beheadings of Egyptian Coptic Christians in Libya," CNN (February 16, 2015) (located at: http://www.cnn.com/2015/02/15/middleeast/isis-video-beheadings-christians/).

15. Patrick Kingsley and Martin Chulov, "Egyptian jihadis pledge allegiance to ISIS," *Guardian* (November 10, 2014) (located at: http://www.theguardian.com/world/2014/nov/10/egyptian-jihadists-pledge-allegiance-isis).

16. Hamdi Alkshali and Steve Almasy, "ISIS leader purportedly accepts Boko Haram's pledge of allegiance," CNN (March 12, 2015) (located at: http://www.cnn.com/2015/03/12/middleeast /isis-boko-haram/).

17. Graphic, "Foreign Fighters Flow into Syria," *Washington Post* (March 8, 2013) (located at: http://www.washingtonpost.com /world/foreign-fighters-flow-to-syria/2015/01/27/7fa56b70-a631-11e4-a7c2-03d37af98440_graphic.html).

18. Ibid.

19. Helene Cooper, Anne Barnard, and Eric Schmitt, "Battered but Unbowed, ISIS Is Still on Offensive," *New York Times* (March 13, 2015) (located at: http://www.nytimes.com/2015 /03/14/world/middleeast/isis-still-on-the-attack-despite-internal-strife-and-heavy-losses.html?_r=0).

CHAPTER THIRTEEN. ISIS IS VULNERABLE

1. Graeme Wood, "What ISIS Really Wants," *Atlantic* (March 2015) (located at: http://www.theatlantic.com/features/archive /2015/02/what-isis-really-wants/384980/).

2. Ibid.

3. Ibid.

4. Ibid.

5. Ibid.

6. Liz Sly, "Islamic State appears to be fraying from within," *Washington Post* (March 8, 2015) (located at: http://www .washingtonpost.com/world/middle_east/the-islamic-state-is-fraying-from-within/2015/03/08/0003a2e0-c276-11e4-a188-8e4971d37a8d_story.html?hpid=z1).

7. Ibid.

8. Helene Cooper, Anne Barnard, and Eric Schmitt, "Battered but Unbowed, ISIS Is Still on Offensive," *New York Times* (March 13, 2015) (located at: http://www.nytimes.com/2015 /03/14/world/middleeast/isis-still-on-the-attack-despite-internal-strife-and-heavy-losses.html?_r=0).

9. https://www.whitehouse.gov/sites/default/files/docs/aumf _02112015.pdf.

10. Ibid.

11. "Exclusive: El-Sisi urges Arab 'ready force' to confront ISIS, questions if US standing by Egypt," Fox News (March 9, 2015) (located at: http://www.foxnews.com/politics/2015/03 /09/exclusive-el-sisi-urges-arab-ready-force-to-confront-isis -questions-if-us/).

12. "Canadians trade fire with ISIS as military waits on possible extension," CBC News (February 12, 2015) (located at: http:// www.cbc.ca/news/politics/canadians-trade-fire-with-isis-as -military-waits-on-possible-extension-1.2955157).

13. Graeme Wood, "'What ISIS Really Wants,' the Response," *Atlantic* (February 24, 2015) (located at: http://www.theatlantic .com/international/archive/2015/02/what-isis-really-wants -reader-response-atlantic/385710/).

14. Ibid.

CHAPTER FOURTEEN. TURKEY: THE POWERFUL WILD CARD

1. For this chapter, we relied heavily on the excellent work of ACLJ Counsel Shaheryar Gill. With his permission, this

chapter draws upon his comprehensive paper, prepared for the March 2015 meetings of the Oxford Centre for the Study of Law and Public Policy.

2. "Turkey Refrains from Supporting Campaign Against ISIL at Paris Meeting," *Today's Zaman* (September 14, 2014) (located at: http://www.todayszaman.com/national_turkey-refrains -from-supporting-campaign-against-isil-at-paris-meeting _358830.html).

3. Ibid.

4. Ibid.

5. Alessandria Masi, "NATO Coalition Against ISIS: Turkey Role Mostly Symbolic," *International Business Times* (September 7, 2014) (located at: http://www.ibtimes.com/nato -coalition-against-isis-turkey-role-mostly-symbolic-1680708).

6. "Pentagon Insists on Turkish Role Against ISIL, Ankara Still Skeptical," *Today's Zaman* (September 14, 2014) (located at: http://www.todayszaman.com/national_pentagon-insists-on -turkish-role-against-isil-ankara-still-skeptical_358719.html).

7. Metin Gurcan, "How and Why Were 46 Turkish Hostages Freed?," *Al-Monitor* (September 21, 2014) (located at: http:// www.al-monitor.com/pulse/originals/2014/09/turkey-iraq -syria-isis-turkish-consulate-hostages-freed.html#).

8. Ashley Fantz, "Who's Doing What in the Coalition Battle Against ISIS," CNN (September 17, 2014) (located at: http:// www.cnn.com/2014/09/14/world/meast/isis-coalition -nations/).

9. "Turkey," *InfoPlease* (located at: http://www.infoplease.com /country/turkey.html?pageno=12). (last visited 10 Feb. 2015).

10. Ibid.

11. Ibid.

12. Berivan Orucoglu, "Turkey Could Focus on ISIS Within Its Own Borders," *New York Times* (October 14, 2014), http:// www.nytimes.com/roomfordebate/2014/10/14/a-missing -ally-against-isis/turkey-could-focus-on-isis-within-its -own-borders.

13. Barney Guiton, "'ISIS Sees Turkey as Its Ally': Former Islamic

State Member Reveals Turkish Army Cooperation," *Newsweek* (November 17, 2014) (located at: http://www.newsweek.com /isis-and-turkey-cooperate-destroy-kurds-former-isis -member-reveals-turkish-282920).

14. Ibid.
15. Ibid.
16. Ibid.
17. Orucoglu, *supra* note 45.
18. Faith Karimi and Talia Kayali, "Dozens of Turkish Hostages Seized By ISIS in Iraq Released Months Later," CNN (October 17, 2014) (located at: http://www.cnn.com/2014/09 /20/world/europe/turkey-iraq-diplomats-freed/).
19. Allen McDuffee, "Activists: ISIS Is Now Launching Attacks from Inside Turkey," *Atlantic* (November 29, 2014) (located at: http://www.theatlantic.com/international/archive/2014/11 /turkey-denies-isis-is-operating-from-its-side-of-the-border /383264/).
20. Id.
21. "ISIS Releases 49 Turkish Hostages Under Circumstances Shrouded in Mystery," *Daily News* (September 20, 2014) (located at: http://www.nydailynews.com/news/world/isis -releases-49-turkish-hostages-report-article-1.1946495).
22. Ibid.
23. Ibid.
24. Catherine Herridge and Lucas Tomlinson, "The Lure of ISIS: Feds Catching More Americans Trying to Aid Terror Groups in Iraq, Syria," Fox News (December 16, 2014) (located at: http://www.foxnews.com/politics/2014/12/16/lure-isis-feds -catching-more-americans-trying-to-aid-terror-groups-in -iraq/).
25. "Report: ISIL Has Sleeper Cells in Ankara, Istanbul, Konya," *Today's Zaman* (September 15, 2014) (located at: http://www .todayszaman.com/national_report-isil-has-sleeper-cells-in -ankara-istanbul-konya_358804.html).
26. Ibid.
27. Ibid.

28. Ibid.

29. McDuffee, *supra* note 52.

30. "Energy Minister Disputes Report, Denies Involvement in ISIL Oil Trade," *Today's Zaman* (September 15, 2014) (located at: http://www.todayszaman.com/national_energy-minister -disputes-report-denies-involvement-in-isil-oil-trade_358763 .html).

31. Amanda Macias and Jeremy Bender, "Here's How the World's Richest Terrorist Group Makes Millions Every Day," *Business Insider* (August 27, 2014) (located at: http://www .businessinsider.com/isis-worlds-richest-terrorist -group-2014-8).

32. Ibid.

33. Ibid.

34. "Energy Minister Disputes Report, Denies Involvement in ISIL Oil Trade," *supra* note 63.

EPILOGUE. THE COST OF STALEMATE

1. Tim McGirk, "A Fight to the Death in Gaza," *Time* (June 12, 2007) (located at: http://content.time.com/time/world/article /0,8599,1632089,00.html).

2. Charlotte Alter, "Netanyahu Tells World Leaders, 'Hamas is ISIS and ISIS is Hamas," *Time* (September 29, 2014) (located at: http://time.com/3445394/netanyahu-un-general-assembly -hamas-abbas/).

3. Nicholas Kristof, "Winds of War in Gaza," *New York Times* (March 7, 2015) (located at: http://www.nytimes.com/2015/03 /08/opinion/sunday/nicholas-kristof-winds-of-war -in-gaza.html?rref=collection%2Fcolumn%2Fnicholas -kristof&contentCollection=opinion&action=click&module= NextInCollection&region=Footer&pgtype=article).